RESTORATION BAWDY

JOHN ADLARD taught in universities in Eastern and Western Europe. He was the author of a study of folklore in William Blake and edited a selection of Blake's poems. His anthology of the work of John Wilmot, Earl of Rochester, is published in the Fyfield series as *The Debt to Pleasure*.

Fyfield*Books* aim to make available some of the great classics of British and European literature in clear, affordable formats, and to restore often neglected writers to their place in literary tradition.

Fyfield*Books* take their name from the Fyfield elm in Matthew Arnold's 'Scholar Gypsy' and 'Thyrsis'. The tree stood not far from the village where the series was originally devised in 1971.

Roam on! The light we sought is shining still.
Dost thou ask proof? Our tree yet crowns the hill,
Our Scholar travels yet the loved hill-side

from 'Thyrsis'

Restoration Bawdy

Poems, Songs and Jests
on the Subject of Sensual Love

Edited with an introduction by
JOHN ADLARD

FyfieldBooks

CARCANET

First published in Great Britain in 1975 as *The Fruit of That Forbidden Tree* by
Carcanet Press Limited
Alliance House
Cross Street
Manchester M2 7AQ

This impression 2003

A CIP catalogue record for this book is available from the British Library
ISBN 1 85754 697 0

The publisher acknowledges financial assistance from
the Arts Council of England

Printed and bound in England by SRP Ltd, Exeter

To the Memory of

Sophia B.	*(5 guineas per night)*
Luci M.	*(gold, a little bit per night)*
Cisely D.	*(1 guinea a night)*
Abigail C.	*(1s. a time)*
Flora A.	*(a guinea a time)*
Elia F.	*(10 guineas a time)*
Phyllis J.	*(1 crown)*
Cybel S.	*(what she can get)*

'good wenches,'

fl. circa 1670.

'Come, come, do not blaspheme this masquerading age . . . By what I've heard, 'tis a pleasant, well-bred, complaisant, free, frolic, good-natured, pretty age; and if you do not like it, leave it to us that do.'

THE GENTLEMAN DANCING-MASTER

INTRODUCTION

Among the less-read works of the amazing Aphra Behn is a poem entitled 'The Golden Age', in which she complains that the concept of Honour 'first did damn' women to 'the sin of shame'. Rochester, whose poems Mrs Behn much admired, also deplored 'huffing Honour', enemy of 'true, generous Love'. So did Sedley and Etherege, his companions.

The theme was far from new in Restoration times. It originated in the famous chorus *O bella età de l'oro* from Tasso's pastoral drama *Aminta,* performed before the Court of Ferrara on the last evening of July, 1573, and perhaps seen in Reading in the following year.[1] The whole play was translated by Henry Reynolds in 1628, but the chorus had already been put into English by Samuel Daniel:

> O happy Golden Age!
> Not for that rivers ran
> With streams of milk, and honey dropped
> from trees;
> Not that the Earth did gage
> Unto the husbandman
> Her voluntary fruits, . . .
>
> But only for that name,
> That idle name of wind,
> That idol of deceit, that empty sound
> Called HONOUR, which became
> The tyrant of the mind
> And so torments our nature without ground,

> Was not yet vainly found,
> Nor yet sad griefs imparts
> Amidst the sweet delights
> Of joyful, am'rous wights;
> Nor were his hard laws known to free-born
> hearts,
> But golden laws like these
> Which Nature wrote — *That's lawful which*
> *doth please.*

This Honour, this idol set up by us, first closed 'the spring of all delight', bringing to an end the time when the naked little virgin was not afraid of man and in lake and river lover played with lover.

'The song of the Golden Age', wrote one Victorian critic, 'has been much admired — rather, it is to be hoped, for its sound than its sentiments.'[2] As recently as 1960 an Italian critic was wondering whether 'this famous page' might be said to be immoral.[3] But in seventeenth-century England, at Court and university, poets appear to have taken it to their hearts. Thomas Carew's 'A Rapture' also has Honour as the villain of the human situation:

> I will enjoy thee now, my Celia, come
> And fly with me to Love's Elysium:
> The giant, Honour, that keeps cowards out
> Is but a masquer, . . .

Similar poems were written by contemporaries, John Hall producing his own 'Rapture' (sometimes carelessly attributed to Cleveland), Thomas Randolph 'A Pastoral Courtship', and William Cartwright 'A Song of Dalliance'. None of them has the range of Carew's 'Rapture'. This, of course, is chiefly concerned with the 'naked, polished ivory'

8

of the girl and particulars of how he means to enjoy her, but it also relates woman's honour to the acquisitiveness of Society and sketches out a revolutionary Elysium:

> The Roman Lucrece there reads the divine
> Lectures of Love's great master, Aretine,
> And knows as well as Lais how to move
> Her pliant body in the act of love.
> To quench the burning ravisher, she hurls
> Her limbs into a thousand winding curls
> And studies artful postures, . . .

Penelope, too, has left her web and displays herself to the youth of Ithaca, preferring 'gamesome nights' to 'dull dreams of the lost Traveller'. Daphne has broken her bark and runs into the embrace of the Sun. Laura lies 'in Petrarch's learned arms', drying his tears. Women are 'unapt for abstinence'.

The year of the Restoration brought a new translation of *Aminta*, the work of John Dancer:

> Most blessed Age of Gold! not cause the floods
> Streamed down pure snow, white milk . . .

This new version of the chorus might well have been commissioned by the Time-Spirit to introduce, after the Commonwealth, the age of Rochester, Buckhurst, Sedley and Etherege. We have most of us been told at school that it was an immoral age and that its licentiousness was a very natural reaction after years of repression under Cromwell. But what we have to consider is a European phenomenon, a seventeenth-century discovery of eroticism seen in those rapturous sonnets on the whipping of beautiful cortesans, by Marcello Giovanetti, Anton Giulio Brignole Sale and other

9

Italians, and in the birth of prose pornography, with *La Putana Errante*, about 1650, and *L'École des Filles* (which Pepys found so exciting) five years before King Charles returned from exile. David Foxon has pointed out that the pornographic prose on sale in Restoration London was 'all continental in origin':

> The repression must be seen in much broader terms — in the Reformation and the Counter-Reformation, which themselves follow earlier 15th-century attempts to do away with those 'abuses' which were safety-valves in an authoritarian society. Dale Underwood in *Etherege and the Seventeenth-Century Comedy of Manners* (New Haven, 1957) relates the change in the tone of the drama to the Europe-wide emergence of 'libertinism' as a fashionable and pervasive mode of thought whose freedom related to religion, politics, and society as well as to sexual life. [4]

Even the career of John Milton shows this need for 'broader terms'. Among his many Italian friends was the poet Antonio Malatesti, who dedicated to him a sequence of jocular sonnets, *La Tina*, in which a countryman woos a country girl with all manner of bawdy puns. Milton seems not to have been in the least offended. 'He continued,' as Christopher Hill reminds us, 'to send friendly greetings to Malatesti, and it has been suggested that a dozen years later he imitated the word-play of Malatesti's bawdy sonnets in his own *Second Defence of the People of England*.' Hill sees him 'by the early 1640s as a man who moved easily in the libertine . . . circles of intellectual London.' [5] And in Book IV of *Paradise Lost* he joins in the condemnation of 'honour':

> Then was not guilty shame, dishonest shame
> Of Nature's works, honour dishonourable, . . .

though at the same time rejecting 'court-amours' and the 'wanton mask'.

The court amours of Rochester and his contemporaries will seem attractive or unattractive according to which anecdotes we choose to tell. The same is of course true of their wenching, which Pepys heard of with a prurient interest he only half admitted. Of that 'store of good wenches' Sedley vows he will enjoy on 'couches, chairs and benches,' a selection were engraved by Hollar, with their names and fees noted beside them. Sophia B — m receives '5 Gui^s p Nig^t', Luci M — n, 'Gold a little Bitt p N^t', Cisely D — v, '1 Gui a N^t', Abigail C. '1^s a time', Flora A — w, 'a Gui a time', Elia F — k, '10 Gui^s a time', Phyllis J — n, '1 Crown', and Cybel Sa — s (described as 'a Str Walker') 'wh^t she can get'. The girls cannot be said to look particularly unhappy, but one may remember Alexander Radcliffe's 'The Poor Whore's Song':

> Once at the Bear in Drury Lane
> The bullies left me for a pawn, [6]
> But I made my party good
> To fifteen guineas and a broad.

or Rochester's account of another wench out of season:

> Poor creature! who, unheard of as a fly,
> In some dark hole must all the winter lie,
> And want and dirt endure a whole half year
> That for one month she tawdry may appear. [7]

'Poor whores are whipped, whilst rich ones ride in coaches,' we are reminded in a mock elegy [8] on the sadistic Sir William, who presided over the floggings at Bridewell and to whom the girls cried out 'Good Sir William, knock!'

11

in hope that with a tap of his hammer he would signal the end of their punishment. Since such horrors are the work of the tyrant Honour, whose slaves and agents sadists are, we may pity the victims and yet at the same time enjoy the songs and poems of young men whose thoughts ran as much as in any generation on 'the embroidered quilt, a bed of jessamine and damask roses . . . and . . . a bedfellow to whose rare entertainment all these are but fools,' who travelled to see (I quote from a farce[9] presented before King and Court at Newmarket) 'the lusty girl of France, the sober German, the plump Dutch fro, the stately dame of Spain, the Roman and spritely Tuscan, the merry Venetian courtesan, the English fair companion, that learns something from every nation.' When will people understand the humanising value of pleasure?

'My dad did so before me,' one of those young men reminds us in a poem by Sedley. Restoration London is generally thought of as being particularly vicious, yet in the pamphlet *Wonderful Strange News from Wood Street Counter,* published in 1642, brothels are mentioned in Turnball Street, Bell Alley, Pickhatch, Covent Garden, Greaping Lane, Tower Hill, St Giles-in-the-Fields, Bloomsbury, Drury Lane, Westminster, Bankside, Cheapside, Lincoln's Inn Fields, together with other, unnamed places 'about London', and one Plain-Dealing asks one Tell-Troth:

> Are there any handsome wenches, fresh virgins, rare didappers? Will they come on, and off, handsomely, will the pretty ducks dive completely? Pox upon thee, my hair stands on end, it has such an itching desire to be resolved.

Tell-Troth replies, 'Fresh lasses, oh yes, there is fresh wenches every night,' and the London of Charles I seems very like the London of Charles II.

Some readers may be surprised to find that this anthology includes both accomplished songs by Dryden and doggerel from the almanacs. But the Restoration was not an age with a marked insulation of classes. One 'B.E., Gent.' tells us that Rochester, 'among other frolics, was not ashamed to keep the gypsies company,'[10] and in 1670 the Queen, the Duchess of Richmond and the Duchess of Buckingham disguised themselves as country lasses to attend a fair near Audley End. Pepys, who set to music a poem by Davenant, also collected ballads sold in the streets, and it seems not to have been noticed that a stanza from one of those street-ballads:

> When first I bid my love goodmorrow,
>   With tear in eye and hand on breast,
> My heart was even drowned in sorrow
>   And I, poor soul, was much oppressed.[11]

inspired Rochester's dialogue between Nell Gwyn, the Duchess of Portsmouth and the King:

> When to the King I bid goodmorrow,
>   With tongue in mouth and hand on tarse,
> Portsmouth may rend her cunt for sorrow
>   And Mazarin may kiss mine arse.

The common people long remembered their pleasure-loving King with a good deal of affection, and liked to think he had moved familiarly among them. In late Victorian times, at a small Clerkenwell public house called the Pickled Egg, a legend still persisted that he had halted there 'during one of his suburban journeys'[12] and eaten one of the eggs from which the place took its name. Till the mid-eighteenth century, at the Three Mariners tavern in Vaux-hall, they showed 'a remarkably high elbowed chair, covered with purple cloth, and ornamented with gilt nails,' where King Charles sat when he 'used, on his water tours with his ladies, to frequent the tavern, to play at chess etc. . .'[13] And one of those ladies, Nell Gwyn, was remembered even longer than the King, in many parts of London, for her humour, her kindness and her frank enjoyment of sexual pleasure.[14]

NOTES

1. Mario Praz: 'Tasso in Inghilterra' (in *Torquato Tasso*, edited by the Ferrara Tasso Festival Committee, Milan, 1957, pages 673-674).

2. E. J. Hasell: *Tasso*, Edinburgh and London, 1882, page 25.

3. Franco Pool: *Desiderio e Realtà Nella Poesia del Tasso*, Padua, 1960, page 51.

4. David Foxon: 'Libertine Literature in England, 1660-1745', III, *The Book Collector*, Autumn 1963, page 305.

5. Christopher Hill: 'Milton the Radical', *Times Literary Supplement*, November 29th, 1974, page 1330.

6. 'To pawn anybody,' according to B.E., Gent.: *A New Dictionary of the Terms Ancient and Modern of the Canting Crew*, London, 1699, is 'to steal away and leave him or them to pay the reckoning.'

7. 'A Letter from Artemisia in the Town to Chloe in the Country'.

8. *Good Sir William, Knock*, broadside, 1693.

9. *Love Lost in the Dark*, London, 1680.

10. Preface to his *New Dictionary of the Terms Ancient and Modern of the Canting Crew*, London, 1699.

11. *The Roxburghe Ballads*, ed. William Chappell, Hertford, 1880, Volume III, page 526.

12. W. J. Pinks: *History of Clerkenwell*, 2nd edition, London, 1881, page 140.

13. Thomas Allen: *History and Antiquities of the Parish of Lambeth*, London, 1826, page 367.

14. I have examined these legends and associations in 'A Note on Nell Gwyn,' *Folklore,* Spring, 1972, pages 61-67.

I

Rinaldo But what think you of the noble Alexander, when he picked up a whore, drank confusion to sobriety and set a whole town o' fire to light 'em to bed together?

Silvio Pick up a whore!

Antonio Who's that talks of whores? A good whore were worth money, boys.

Rinaldo Ay, where are they? Where are the wenches?

THE CITY RAMBLE

1   There was an old man had an acre of land,
        He sold it for five pound a;
    He went to the tavern and drank it all out,
        Excepting half a crown a,
    And as he came home he met with a wench
        And asked her whether she was willing
    To go to the tavern and spend eighteen pence
        And fuck for the other odd shilling.

Merry Drollery Complete, 1691

2   If the season proves unkind
        The bees will yield no honey,
    And if you'll lie with me tonight
        You must give me your money;
    And under the moss the mine grows,
        And under the mine the money,
                    And under the waist
                    The belly is placed,
                    And under that
                    I know not what,
    But I think they do call it a cony.

New Academy of Compliments, 1671

3   I am a lusty, lively lad
        Arrived at one and twenty;
    My father left me all he had —
        Both gold and silver plenty.
    Now he's in grave I will be brave;
        The ladies shall adore me;
    I'll court and kiss — what hurt's in this?
        My dad did so before me.

    My father, to get my estate,
        Though selfish yet was slavish;

18

I'll spend it at another rate
   And be as lewdly lavish.
From madmen, fools and knaves he did
   Litigiously receive it.
If so he did, justice forbid
   But I to such should leave it.

Then I'll to Court, where Venus' sport
   Doth revel it in plenty,
And deal with all, both great and small,
   From twelve to five and twenty:
In playhouses I'll spend my days,
   For there are store of misses.
Ladies, make room, behold, I come
   To purchase many kisses.

Sir Charles Sedley

4 There's no man more happy than he
That's free from a troublesome wife,
A whore at command
And a glass in his hand
Are the three chief blessings of life.

The young and the old mun to't, mun to't,
The young and the old mun to't.
The young ones will learn to do't, to do't,
And the old ones forget not to do't.

George Powell

5 Happy is the man that takes delight
   In banqueting his senses,
That drinks all day and then at night
   The height of joy commences.

With bottles armed we stand our ground —

Full bumpers crown our blisses —
Then roar and sing the streets around
    In serenading misses.

By blessings free and unconfined
    We prove without reproaches
There's no bliss like a frolic mind
    Or pleasures like debauches;

Whilst rambling thus new joys we reap
    In charms of love and drinking;
Insipid fops lie drowned in sleep
    And the cuckold he lies thinking.

Tom D'Urfey

6 Since death on all lays his impartial hand,
    And all resign at his command,
    The Stoic too, as well as I,
    With all his gravity must die:
    Let's wisely manage the last span,
    The momentary life of man,
    And still in pleasure's circle move,
    Giving t'your friends the days, and all our
        nights to love.

Chorus

Thus, thus, whilst we are here, let's perfectly live,
And taste all the pleasures that nature can give;
Fresh heat when life's fading our wine will inspire,
And fill all our veins with a noble desire.

When we are sapless, old and impotent,
Then we shall grieve for youth misspent:
Wine and woman only can
Cherish the drooping heart of man.

Let's drink until our blood o'erflows
Its channels and luxurious grows;
Then when our whores have drained each vein,
And the thin mass fresh spirits crave, let's drink again.

Chorus — Thus, thus, &c,

The happy king, whom heaven itself called wise,
Saw all was vanity but dice;
His active mind, ever in quest of bliss,
Surveyed all things, and stuck to this.
Myriads of harlots round him strove,
Some sung, whilst others acted love.
Who shall our frailty then condemn,
Since one by heaven inspired left heaven to
      follow them?

Chorus — Thus, thus, &c,

Sir George Etherege

7 Drink about till the day find us;
      These are pleasures that will last;
Let no foolish passion blind us,
      Joys of love they fly too fast.

Maids are long ere we can win 'um
      And our passions waste the while,
In a beer-glass we'll begin 'um,
      Let some beau take th' other toil.

Yet we will have store of good wenches,
      Though we venture fluxing for 't,
Upon couches, chairs and benches,
      To outdo them at the sport,

Joining thus both mirth and beauty,

21

To make up our full delight:
In wine and love we pay our duty
To each friendly coming night.

Sir Charles Sedley

8 Let Taffy go seek for his bliss in a leek
And Teag in hot isquebagh slobber,
Jocky be doing with oatcakes and sowing,
And sup up their brave, bonny clabber.

But let misses and gallants make use of
their talents;
To be wise is to love and be drunk,
For drink and that same will get you a name
When your health and estates are all sunk.

Let sullen old men keep their besom beards clean,
Let slaves strive for honour and riches,
Let widgeons debate our Religion and State,
And matrons be sober as witches.

Chorus — But let misses &c.

Let's drink and be clapped till our shin-bone
sore scraped
And gems deck our faces all over,
Till palsies and cramps make our eyes shine like lamps,
For such is the true drunken lover.

Chorus — Yet let misses &c.

Thomas Duffett

9 Reader, beneath this marble stone
Saint Valentine's adopted son,
Bennet the bawd, now lies alone.

Here lies alone the amorous spark
Who was used to lead them in the dark
Like beasts by pairs into the Ark.

If men of honour would begin
He'd ne'er stick out at any sin,
For he was still for sticking 't in.

If Justice chiefest of the Bench
Had an occasion for a wench,
His reverend flames 'twas he could quench.

And for his son and heir apparent
He could perform as good an errand
Without a tipstaff or a warrant.

Over the clergy [he] had such a lock
That he could make a spiritual frock
Fly off at sight of temporal smock.

Like will i' the wisp still up and down
He led the wives of London Town,
To lodge with squires of high renown,

While they (poor fools) being unaware,
Did find themselves in mansion fair
Near Leicester Fields or James's Square.

Thus worthy Bennet was employed: —
At last he held the door so wide
He caught a cold, so coughed and died.

Alexander Radcliffe

10   A young girl that's newly come to town
And in her russet wanders up and down
Ventures her maidenhead for half a crown.

John Leanerd

11 I am a brave lass and I travelled about
with a fa la la le le la lero
And behaved myself bravely upon the road,
with a fa la la le le la lero
And was welcome to every place where I did come
And many a brave gallant did look me upon;
But I have a fine trick for to play with my own.
with a fa la la le le la lero
I prospered so well that to London I came,
with a fa la la le le la lero
For that is a place to get a good name;
with a fa la la le le la lero
I have my silk gowns and my scarfs to wear
And many a brave gallant doth call me his dear;
They see I am so willing to let out my ware.
with a fa la la le le la lero
My money comes easily into my lap;
with a fa la la le le la lero
I am a sound country girl and give no one a clap.
with a fa la la le le la lero
Five crowns at a time I have in my hand,
And all for fine kisses they have at command;
This is gallant profit I do understand.
with a fa la la le le la lero
I'll send for my sister, she shall be of my trade —
with a fa la la le le la lero
She's as pretty as I am and is as well made —
with a fa la la le le la lero
And not live in the country, to abide so much itch,
But come up to London and learn to be rich.
What if now and then she do venture a touch?
with a fa la la le le la lero
Nothing venture, nothing have.
with a fa la la le le la lero

I am all for brave gamesters, I scorn a poor knave
　　with a fa la la le le la lero

Broadside, circa **1680**

12　You gallants know, a fresh wench of sixteen
　　May drive the trade in honest bombasine
　　And never want good custom, should she be
　　In a back room two or three stories high;
　　But such a beauty as has long been known,
　　Though not decayed, but to perfection grown,
　　Must, if she mean to thrive in this lewd town,
　　Wear points, laced petticoats and a rich gown.
　　Her lodgings, too, must with her dress agree,
　　Be hung with damask, or with tapestry,
　　Have china, cabinets, and a great glass,
　　To strike respect into an am'rous ass.
　　Without the help of stratagems and arts
　　An old acquaintance cannot touch your hearts.

Sir George Etherege

13　Chloe's the brightest of her sex;
　　　'Tis well her heart is tender:
　　How would those killing eyes perplex
　　　If virtue did defend her!

　　But Nature's merciful and kind,
　　　Loves not to vex but please us,
　　[And] to her matchless beauty joined
　　　A boundless will to ease us.

Harleian MS. 6914

14　She was so exquisite a whore
　　　　That in the belly of her mother

25

She turned her cunt so right before
        Her father fucked them both together.

> *The Works of the Earls of Rochester,
> Roscommon and Dorset,* 1718; but
> identified by Ernest J. Moncada (*Notes
> and Queries,* March, 1964) as a joke
> of wide European currency; he quotes
> a Spanish version.

15 Oh, she is, she is a matchless piece,
    Though all the world may woo her;
    Not Golden Shower nor Golden Fleece
    Is price enough to do her.

George Powell

16 If any man do want a house,
    Be he prince, baronet or squire,
    Or peasant, hardly worth a louse,
        I can fit his desire.

    I have a tenement the which
    I'm sure can fit them all;
    'Tis seated near a stinking ditch,
        Some call it Cunny Hall.

    It stands close by Cunny Alley
    At foot of Belly Hill.
    This house is freely to be let
        To whom soever will.

    For term of life or years or days
    I'll let this pleasant bower,
    Nay, rather than a tenant want
        I'll let it for an hour.

26

About it grows a lofty wood
Will save you from the sun;
Well watered 'tis, for throughout
        A pleasant stream doth run.

If hot, you there may cool yourself,
If cool, you'll there find heat;
For greatest 'tis not too little
        For least 'tis not too great.

I must confess my house is dark,
Be it by night or day,
But when you're once but got therein
        You cannot lose your way.

And when you are in go boldly on,
As fast as e'er you can,
For if you go to the end thereof
        You go where ne'er did man.

But though my house be deep and dark,
'T has many a man made merry
And in't much liquor has been spent
        More precious than the sherry.

Thus if you like my Cunny Hall
Your house-room shall be good,
For such a temper as you find
        Burns neither coal nor wood,

For if it rain or freeze or snow —
To speak I dare be bold —
If you keep your nose within the door
        You ne'er shall feel the cold.

But I must covenant with him
That takes this house of mine,

Whether it be for term of life
      Or else for shorter time,

See that you dress it twice a day
And rub it round about,
And if you do dislike of this
      I'll seek a new tenant out.

               New Academy of Compliments, 1671

17 *Quaker*   My friend, thy beauty seemeth good.
              We Righteous have our failings;
              I'm flesh and blood, methinks I could,
              Wert thou but free from ailings.

   Harlot   Believe me, sir, I'm newly broached
              And never have been in yet;
              I vow and swear I ne'er was touched
              By man till this day sen'night.

   Quaker   Then prithee friend, now prithee do,
              Nay, let us not defer it,
              And I'll be kind to thee when thou
              Hast laid the evil spirit.

   Harlot   I vow I won't, indeed I shan't,
              Unless I've money first, sir;
              For if I ever trust a saint
              I wish I may be cursed, sir.

   Quaker   I cannot like the Wicked say
              I love thee and adore thee,
               And therefore thou wilt make me pay,
              So here is sixpence for thee.

   Harlot   Confound you for a stingy Whig!
              D'ye think I live by stealing?

Farewell, you Puritanic prig,
I scorn to take your shilling.

Penkethman's Jests, 1721

18 Walking abroad in a morning
Where Venus herself was adorning,
I heard a bird sing to welcome the Spring,
Their music so sweetly according.

I listened unto them;
Methought a voice did summon:
I spied an old whore and a lusty young rogue
Together as they sat a-wooing.

She tickled him under the sides
To make their courage coming,
She hoisted her thighs and she twinkled her eyes:
'Twas a dainty, fine, curious old woman.

If Venus and Mars so stout
Had joined together in battle,
There could not have been more claps and more
bangs,
For he made her old buttocks rattle.

She gave him a lift for his thrust
And catched him as he was a-coming;
She gave him five shillings to make a recruit.
And was not this a fine, lusty old woman?

Merry Drollery Complete, 1691

19 As I came up by Harpenden
And straight to Watton Town,
And there I met a pretty wench
That looked like Lay-me-down.

At Watton Town-End, at Watton Town-End,
At every door there stands a whore,
At Watton Town-End.

The frigate's name was Thunderbolt,
   Her sails were all of silk;
Her tackling was of silver twist,
   Her colour like the milk.
At Watton Town-End, at Watton Town-End,
At every door there stands a whore,
At Watton Town-End.

Her planks were all of ivory,
   Her bottom beaten gold,
Her deck was alabaster pure;
   She looked brisk and bold.
At Watton Town-End, at Watton Town-End,
At every door there stands a whore,
At Watton Town-End.

Her head was gilded o'er and o'er,
   Her wanton flag did fly,
And I was mad to be on board,
   So much a fool was I.
At Watton Town-End, at Watton Town-End,
At every door there stands a whore,
At Watton Town-End.

She seemed a stately pleasure boat,
   With tempting good attire,
But little knew that (under deck)
   Her gun room was on fire.
At Watton Town-End, at Watton Town-End,
At every door there stands a whore,
At Watton Town-End.

I lodged with her, I laid her down,
    I slept with her all night:
I supped upon a cony fat
    Whose gravy was delight,
At Watton Town-End, at Watton Town-End,
At every door there stands a whore,
At Watton Town-End.

She gave to me a syrup sweet
    Was in her placket box,
But ere three minutes went about
    It proved the French pox.
At Watton Town-End, at Watton Town-End,
At every door there stands a whore,
At Watton Town-End.

This fireship she did blow me up,
    As my *effigies* shows,
And all may read upon my face
    The loss of teeth and nose.
At Watton Town-End, at Watton Town-End,
At every door there stands a whore,
At Watton Town-End.

Now as I walk along the streets
    They gaze upon my face,
And everyone that looks at me
    Salutes me with disgrace.
At Watton Town-End, at Watton Town-End,
At every door there stands a whore,
At Watton Town-End.

By me beware then, gentlemen,
    From King to country clown,
And when you see a pretty wench,
    Remember Lay-me-down.

31

At Watton Town-End, at Watton Town-End,
At every door there stands a whore,
At Watton Town-End.

Broadside, circa 1670

20 *The humble Address of the Ladies of Pleasure.*

We, your Majesty's most loyal and dutiful subjects,
the Ladies of Pleasure in the several seraglios of
Moorfields, Whetstone's Park, Lukener's Lane, Dog
and Bitch Yard, and the rest of the stews and cony-
burrows in and about the virtuous Palace of Whitehall
and the Cities of London and Westminster, being
daily sensible of the great advantage we have reaped,
under your Majesty's easy government, from the
playhouses, masques, balls, serenades, Hyde Park and
St James' night revels, publicly recommended and
honoured by your Majesty's presence, and for the
great licence and privilege we have enjoyed under
your Majesty's Justices of the Peace, no ways inferior
to those of the ladies of Rome or Venice, whereby
those foolish things called wives are grown unfashion-
able and the keeping of a miss the principal character
of a modish, well-bred gentleman: And having no less
resentments of the honours some of our profession
have received from your Majesty, in being promoted
. . . to great titles . . . we do humbly beg leave to
return our hearty thanks to your Majesty for all the
said blessings . . . And we humbly assure ourselves of
your Majesty's acceptance of this our zeal, which we
will never be wanting to express as long as we are able
to wag our tails, from the hands of our chiefs, the
Duchess of Portsmouth and Madam Gwyn, whom we
have prevailed with to present the same . . .

Dyce M S. 43

21 *Nell Gwyn* When to the king I bid good morrow,
        With tongue in mouth and hand on tarse,
        Portsmouth may rend her cunt for sorrow
        And Mazarın may kiss mine arse.

Duchess of Portsmouth
        When England's monarch's on my belly,
        With prick in cunt, though double
                        crammed,
        Fart of mine arse for small whore Nelly
        And great whore Mazarin be damned.

The King When on Portsmouth's lap I lay my head
        And Knight does sing her bawdy song,
        I envy not George Porter's bed
        Nor the delights of Madam Long.

The People
        Now heavens preserve our faith's defender
        From Paris plots and Roman cunt,
        From Mazarin, that new pretender,
        And from that *politique*, Grammont.

                    John Wilmot,
                Earl of Rochester

22 When Portsmouth did from England fly,
    To follow her Vendôme,
Then all along the gallery
    Our monarch did make moan:
' Oh [Barillon], in charity,
    Send me my old whore home!

' This nymph, too foolish and unkind,
    Does a wandering knight pursue
And sadly leaves a King behind,
    Too constant and too true.

Ye Gods! When you made Cupid blind
You should have lamed him too.'

Chetham MS. Mun.A.4.14

23 *At the Royal Coffee House at Charing Cross are these following goods to be sold in small lots, March 20th, 1680 . . .*

Two dozen of French wenches, the one half to dance naked before his majesty to keep him still in the Protestant Religion, the other behind to bring him over to the Duke of York's religion. 30000l. a dozen, to advance a guinea and a half each bidding.

Dyce MS 43

24 My mistress is a shittlecock,
    Composed of cork and feather;
Each battledore sets on her dock
    And bumps her on the leather;
But cart her off which way you will,
    She will recoil to another still.
                Fa, la, la, la, la, la.

My mistress is a tennis-ball,
    Composed of cotton fine,
She is often struck against the wall
    And bandied under line,
But if you will her mind fulfil
    You must pop her in the hazard still.
                Fa, la, la, la, la, la.

My mistress is a nightingale,
    So sweetly she can sing,
She is as fair as Philomel,
    The daughter of a king,

And in the darksome nights so thick
She loves to lean against a prick.
Fa, la, la, la, la, la.

My mistress is a ship of war
    With shot discharged at her;
The poop hath inferred many a scar
    Even both by wind and water,
But as she grapples at the last
She drowns the man, pulls down her mast.
Fa, la, la, la, la, la.

My mistress is a virginal
    And little cost will string her;
She's often reared against a wall
    For every man to finger;
But, to say truth, if you will her please
You must run divisions on her keys.
Fa, la, la, la, la, la.

My mistress is a cony fine;
    She's of the softest skin,
And if you please to open her
    The best part lies within,
And in her cony-burrow may
Two tumblers and a ferret play.
Fa, la, la, la, la, la.

My mistress is the Moon so bright;
    I wish that I could win her;
She never walks but in the night
    And bears a man within her
Which on his back bears pricks and thorns,

And once a month she brings him horns.
                    Fa, la, la, la, la, la.

My mistress is a tinder-box —
        Would I had such a one!
Her steel endureth many a knock
        Both by the flint and stone,
And if you stir the tinder much
The match will fire at every touch.
                    Fa, la, la, la, la, la.

My mistress is a Puritan:
        She will not swear an oath,
But for to lie with any man
        She is not very loath.
Put pure to pure and there's no sin;
There's nothing lost that enters in.
                    Fa, la, la, la, la, la.

But why should I my mistress call
        A shittlecock or bauble,
A ship of war or tennis-ball,
        Which things be variable?
But to commend I'll say no more —
My mistress is an arrant WHORE.
                    Fa, la, la, la, la, la.

                    Merry Drollery Complete, 1691

25 That beauty I adored before
        I now as much despise:
    'Tis money only makes the whore,
        She that for love with her crony lies
    Is chaste: But that's the whore that kisses for prize.

    Let Jove with gold his Danae woo;
        It shall be no rule for me:
    Nay, 't may be I may do so too
        When I'm as old as he;
    Till then I'll never hire the thing that's free.

    If coin must your affection imp,
        Pray get some other friend;
    My pocket ne'er shall be my pimp:
        I never that intend,
    Yet can be noble too, if I see they mend.

    Since loving was a liberal art,
        How canst thou trade for gain?
    The pleasure is on your part;
        'Tis we men take the pain,
    And being so, must women have the gain?

    No, no, I'll never farm your bed,
        Nor your smock-tenant be:
    I hate to rent your white and red;
        You shall not let your love to me;
    I court a mistress, not a landlady.

    A pox take him that first set up
        Th' excise of flesh and skin;
    And since it will no better be,

Let's both to kiss begin.
To kiss freely: if not, you may go spin.

The Westminster Drollery, 1671

26 These London wenches are so stout
    They care not what they do;
They will not let you have a bout
    Without a crown or two.

They double their chops and curl their locks,
    Their breaths perfume they do;
Their tails are peppered with the pox,
    And that you're welcome to.

But give me the buxom country lass,
    Hot piping from the cow,
That will take a touch upon the grass,
    Ay, many, and thank you too.

Her colour's as fresh as the rose in June,
    Her temper as kind as a dove;
She'll please the swain with a wholesome tune
    And freely give her love.

*Wit and Mirth: or Pills to
Purge Melancholy*, 1699 − 1700

27 The pot and the pipe,
    The cup and the can
Have quite undone, quite undone,
    Many a man;
The hawk and the hound,
    The dice and the whore

Have quite undone, quite undone
    Many a score
Quite undone, quite undone
    Many a more.

New Academy of Compliments, 1671

28 He that leaves his wine for boxes and dice
    Or his wench for fear of mishaps,
May he beg all his days, cracking of lice,
    And die in conclusion of claps.

Sir George Etherege

II

Prue   What makes 'em go away, Mr Tattle? What do they mean, do you know?

Tattle   Yes, my dear, — I think I can guess; — but hang me if I know the reason of it.

Prue   Come, must not we go too?

Tattle   No, no, they don't mean that.

Prue   No! What then? What should you and I do together?

Tattle   I must make love to you, pretty miss; will you let me make love to you?

Prue   Yes, if you please.

LOVE FOR LOVE

29 Young I am and yet unskilled
    How to make a lover yield:
    How to keep or how to gain,
    When to love and when to feign.

    Take me, take me, some of you
    While I yet am young and true,
    Ere I can my soul disguise,
    Heave my breasts and roll my eyes.

    Stay not till I learn the way
    How to lie and to betray;
    He that has me first is blest,
    For I may deceive the rest.

    Could I find a blooming youth,
    Full of love and full of truth,
    Brisk and of a jaunty mien,
    I should long to be fifteen.

John Dryden

30 You said that I was loved, you knew by who,
    And if I named her you would tell me true.
    I rudely asked if 'twere myself you meant,
    And you as kindly smiled consent.
                Never was man so blessed
                Or love so kind expressed,
    For what I most did value cost me least.

    Then tell me, fair one, thou who art
    Both medicine and physician of my heart,
    Who in compassion to my fainting health
    Kindly prescribed thyself;
                Tell me, I say, what 'tis
                That thus obstructs my bliss
    And I arrive no further than a kiss.

You love and you confess. Forbear to name
Those phantoms, honour, conscience, fear or shame:
God ne'er intended anything should prove
A hindrance to Love.
           They're things designed
           To keep the vulgar blind
And show a distance, not debase a noble mind.

I'm none of Plato's gazing Sons of Art,
Whose eyes were only guardians of their heart,
Stared out their time in one impertinence
And damned for to oblige one sense.
           What 'tis I'd do
           As well as I you know,
Fain would, and yet a feigned resistance show.

Open thy gates and let the victor in,
For mutual love is always void of sin,
And you like rendered towns claim this alone:
That though the arms you do lay down
           And yield to the mighty foe,
           March off you always do
With flying colours and triumphant show.

Oliver Le Neve

31 Leave this gaudy, gilded stage,
From custom more than use frequented,
Where fools of either sex and age
Crowd to see themselves presented.
To Love's theatre, the bed,
Youth and Beauty fly together,
And act so well it may be said
The laurel there was due to either.
'Twixt strifes of Love and war the difference lies in this:

When neither overcomes, Love's triumph greater is.

John Wilmot, Earl of Rochester

32 I could love thee till I die,
    Would'st thou love me modestly,
    And ne'er press, whilst I live,
    For more than willingly I would give:
       Which should sufficient be to prove
       I'd understand the art of love.

    I hate the thing is called enjoyment.
    Besides, it is a dull employment;
    It cuts off all that's life and fire
    From that which may be termed desire,
       Just like the bee whose sting is gone
       Converts its owner to a drone.

    I love a youth will give me leave
    His body in my arms to wreathe,
    To press him gently and to kiss,
    To sigh and look with eyes that wish
       For what, if I could once obtain,
       I would neglect with flat disdain.

    I'd give him liberty to toy
    And play with me, and count it joy;
    Our freedom should be full complete
    And nothing wanting but the feat.
       Let's practice, then, and we shall prove
       These are the only sweets of love.

John Wilmot, Earl of Rochester

33 Phillis at first seemed much afraid,
    Much afraid, much afraid,
    Yet when I kissed she soon repaid.

Could you but see, could you but see
What I did more, you'd envy me,
What I did more, you'd envy me,
You'd envy me.

We then so sweetly were employed,
The height of pleasure we enjoyed.
Could you but see, could you but see,
You'd say so too, if you saw me,
You'd say so too, if you saw me,
If you saw me.

She was so charming, kind and free,
None ever could more happy be.
Could you but see, could you but see,
Where I was, there you'd wish to be,
Where I was, there you'd wish to be,
You'd wish to be.

All the delights we did express,
Yet craving more still to possess.
Could you but see, could you but see,
You'd curse and say, 'Why was't not me?'
You'd curse and say, 'Why was't not me?
Why was't not me?'

Ladies, if how to love you'd know,
She can inform what we did do;
But could you see, but could you see,
You'd cry aloud, 'The next is me!'
You'd cry aloud, 'The next is me!
The next is me!'

Wit and Mirth: or,
Pills to Purge Melancholy,
1699-1700

34 Virgins are like the silver finny race,
     Of slippery kind, and fishes seem in part.
  Lovers, look to't: be sure to bait the place,
     Lay well your hooks, and cast your nets with art.

Philip Ayres

35 Lute, I entreat thee to complain
To her that doth my love disdain,
And when thy mistress cometh home
Tell her here hath been one
Would (if she had not thought it much)
Have given her a gentle touch.

Cupid's Posies, 1674

36   A lass, espying a young man's testicles hang out of his breeches, that were broken in the seat, asked him, with a seeming or real ignorance, what it was. 'It is my purse,' quoth he. 'Thy purse?' quoth she. 'Then I am sure my purse is cut.'

Nugae Venales, 1686

37   She's so bonny and brisk
      How she'd curvet and frisk
If a man were once mounted upon her!
     Let me have but a leap
     Where 'tis wholesome and cheap,
And a fig for your person of honour.

Sir George Etherege

38 *Enter Airy, dancing and singing.*
     When the kind, wanton hour
     Gave me into his power,
     He never trembled more

To go on duty
When he, to win renown,
Scaled a proud, lofty town,
As to lay gently down
   A yielding beauty.

John Crowne

39 And here and there I had her,
And everywhere I had her;
Her toy was such that every touch
Would make a lover madder.

For he that would have a wench kind
   Ne'er smugs up himself like a ninny,
But plainly tells her his mind
   And tickles her first with a guinea.

Sir George Etherege

40 Kind lovers, love on,
Lest the world be undone
   And mankind be lost by degrees,
For if all from their loves
Should go wander in groves
   There soon would be nothing but trees.

John Crowne

41 If she be not as kind as fair,
   But peevish and unhandy,
Leave her, she's only worth the care
   Of some spruce jack-a-dandy.
I would not have thee such an ass,
   Hadst thou ne'er so much leisure,
To sigh and whine for such a lass
   Whose pride's above her pleasure.

47

Make much of every buxom girl
  Which needs but little courting;
Her value is above the pearl
  That takes delight in sporting.

Sir George Etherege

42 *Phillis*   Prithee tell me, Amarillis,
                Why each night you sigh and groan.

Amarillis   If you'd know the truth, my Phillis,
                'Tis because I lie alone:
                Damon he falls off from wooing
                And I'm very much afraid,
                'Spite of all we have been doing,
                I shall live and die a maid.

Phillis   My Alexis, too, grows cold,
                That was once so full of fire,

Amarillis   Surely Phillis we grow old,
                Or they longer would admire.

Phillis   Old, Amarillis? pray, what do you mean?
                You know your own self I am not thirteen.
                If he looks for a younger wife, e'en let
                              him find one;
                And if he proves surly, I'll seek out a
                              kind one.
                I'll not sigh for men in a place where
                              there's plenty;
                'Twill be hard if I find not one lover in
                              twenty.

Amarillis   'Tis bravely resolved. I'll follow that rule
                And let silly Damon alone.

| *Phillis* | Nor shall coy Alexis find me such a fool, |
| | To love when I find he has done. |

| *Amarillis* | Therefore we'll resolve no longer to pine. |

| *Phillis* | Not I, by my troth, Amarillis. |

| *Amarillis* | If Strephon loves better than Damon he's |
| | mine. |

| *Phillis* | And he that loves me shall have Phillis. |

George Powell

43 Love's a hawk and stoops apace:
      We all hurry
      For the quarry,
Though the sport ends with the chase.

Peter Motteux

44 Sylvia the fair, in the bloom of fifteen,
Felt an innocent warmth as she lay on the green;
She had heard of a pleasure and something she guessed
By the touzing and tumbling and touching her breast;
She saw the men eager, but was at a loss
What they meant by their sighing and kissing so close,
      By their praying and whining
      And clasping and twining
      And panting and wishing
      And sighing and kissing
      And sighing and kissing so close.

'Ah', she cried, 'ah, for a languishing maid
In a country of Christians to die without aid!
Not a Whig, or a Tory, or Trimmer at least,
Or a Protestant parson or Catholic priest,

To instruct a young virgin that is at a loss
What they meant by their sighing and kissing so close!
    By their praying and whining
    And clasping and twining
    And panting and wishing
    And sighing and kissing
    And sighing and kissing so close.'

Cupid in shape of a swain did appear;
He saw the sad wound and in pity drew near,
Then showed her his arrow and bid her not fear,
For the pain was no more than a maiden may bear.
When the balm was infused she was not at a loss
What they meant by their sighing and kissing so close,
    By their praying and whining
    And clasping and twining
    And panting and wishing
    And sighing and kissing
    And sighing and kissing so close.

John Dryden

45 Phillis, this early zeal assuage;
      You over-act your part:
  The Martyrs at your tender age
      Gave heaven but half their heart.

  Old men till past the pleasure ne'er
      Declaim against the sin;
  'Tis early to begin to fear
      The Devil at fifteen.

  The world to Youth is too severe
      And, like a treacherous light,
  Beauty, the actions of the fair,
      Exposes to their sight.

And yet this world, as old as 'tis,
   Is oft deceived by't too;
Kind combinations seldom miss —
   Let's try what we can do.

                   Sir Charles Sedley

46 *Daphnis*   See first yon cypress grove, a shade
                         from noon.
   Chloris   Browse on, my goats, for I'll be with you
                         soon.
   Daphnis   Feed well, my bulls, to whet your appetite,
           That each may take a lusty leap at night.
   Chloris   What do you mean, uncivil as you are,
           To touch my breasts and leave my bosom
                         bare?
   Daphnis   These pretty bubbies first I make my own.
   Chloris   Pull out your hand, I swear, or I shall
                         swoon.
   Daphnis   Why does thy ebbing blood forsake thy face?
   Chloris   Throw me at least upon a cleaner place.
           My linen ruffled and my waistcoat soiling —
           What do you think new clothes were made
                         for? spoiling?
   Daphnis   I'll lay my lambskins underneath thy back.
   Chloris   My headgear's off. What filthy work you
                         make!
   Daphnis   To Venus first I'll lay these off'rings by . . .
   Chloris   Nay, first look round, that nobody be nigh:
           Methinks I hear a whisp'ring in the grove.
   Daphnis   The cypress trees are telling tales of love.
   Chloris   You tear off all, behind me and before me,
           And I'm as naked as my mother bore me.

           John Dryden (after Theocritus)

47   Let us drink and be merry, dance, joke and rejoice
      With claret and sherry, theorbo and voice;
      The changeable world to our joy is unjust,
      All treasure uncertain — then down with your dust!
        In frolics dispose your pounds, shillings and pence,
        For we shall be nothing a hundred years hence.

      We'll kiss and be free with Nan, Betty and Philly,
      Have oysters and lobsters and maids by the belly.
      Fish-dinners will make a lass spring like a flea;
      Dame Venus (Love's Goddess) was born of the sea;
        With her and with Bacchus we'll tickle the sense,
        For we shall be past it a hundred years hence.

      Your most beautiful bit that hath all eyes upon her,
      That her honesty sells for a hogo of Honour,
      Whose lightness and brightness doth shine in such
                      splendour
      That none but the stars are thought fit to attend her,
        Though now she be pleasant and sweet to the sense,
        Will be damnable mouldy a hundred years hence.

      Then why should we turmoil in cares and in fears,
      Turn all our tranquillity to sighs and tears?
      Let's eat, drink and play till the worms do corrupt us;
      'Tis certain that *post mortem nulla voluptas*.
        Let's deal with our damsels, that we may from
                      thence
        Have broods to succeed us a hundred years hence.

Thomas Jordan

48   Pretty nymph, why always blushing?
      If thou lov'st why art thou so coy?
    In thy cheeks these roses flushing
      Show thee fearful of thy joy.

What is man, that thou should'st dread
To change with him a maidenhead?

At first all virgins fear to do it
    And but trifle away their time,
And still unwilling to come to it,
    In foolish whining spend their time;
But when they once have found the way,
Then they are for it night and day.

Wit's Cabinet, circa 1700

49 I loved a lass, alas my folly!
        Was full of her coy disdaining;
    I courted her thus: 'What shall I, sweet Molly,
        Do for thy dear love's obtaining?'
    At length I did dally so long with my Molly
        That Molly, for all her feigning,
    Had got such a mountain above her valley
        That Molly came home complaining.

The New Help to Discourse, 1669

50 He that will court a wench that is coy,
        That is proud, that is peevish and antic,
    Let him be careless to sport and toy
        And as peevish as she is frantic.
                Laugh at her and slight her,
                Flatter her, spite her,
    Rail and commend her again —
                It is the way to woo her,
                If you mean to come close to her:
    Such girls will love such men.

He that will court a wench that is mild,
    That is soft and kind of behaviour,

53

Let him kindly woo her,
    Not roughly come to her —
'Tis the way to win her favour.
    Give her kisses plenty,
    She'll take them were they twenty;
Stroke her and kiss her again —
    It is the way to woo her,
    If that you mean to come close to her:
Such girls do love soft men.

He that will court a wench that is mad,
  That will squeak and cry out if you handle her,
    Let him kiss and fling
    Till he make the house ring —
'Tis the only way to tame her.
    Take her up and touze her,
    Salute her and rouse her,
Then kiss her and please her again —
    It is the way to woo her,
    If that you mean to come close to her:
Mad girls do love mad men.

Windsor Drollery, 1672

51 Come, child, let us kiss — hang dull, silly wooing;
'Tis time, like our betters, we two should be doing,
Kind Fate still assigns, as a custom that's common,
To the mistress the master, the man to the woman.

Peter Motteux

52 This is shy and pretty,
And this is wild and witty;
If either stayed
Till she died a maid,
I' faith, 'twould be a great pity.

Sir George Etherege

53 Young Corydon and Phillis
        Sat in a lovely grove,
    Contriving crowns of lilies,
        Repeating tales of love
    And something else, but what I dare not name.

    But as they were a playing
        She ogled so the swain,
    It saved her plainly saying,
        'Let's kiss to ease our pain
    And something else, but what I dare not name.'

    A thousand times he kissed her,
        Laying her on the green,
    But as he further pressed her
        A pretty leg was seen,
    And something else, but what I dare not name.

    So many beauties viewing
        His ardour still increased,
    And greater joys pursuing
        He wandered o'er her breast
    And something else, but what I dare not name.

    A last effort she trying
        His passion to withstand
    Cried — but 'twas faintly crying —
        'Pray take away your hand
    And something else, but what I dare not name.'

    Young Corydon, grown bolder,
        The minutes would improve.
    'This is the time,' he told her,
        'To show you how I love
    And something else, but what I dare not name.'

The nymph seemed almost dying,
   Dissolved in amorous heat;
She kissed and told him, sighing,
   'My dear, your love is great
And something else, but what I dare not name.'

But Phillis did recover
   Much sooner than the swain.
She, blushing, asked her lover,
   'Shall we not kiss again?
And something else, but what I dare not name.'

Thus Love, his revels keeping
   Till nature at a stand,
From talk they fell to sleeping,
   Holding each other's hand
And something else, but what I dare not name.

Sir Charles Sedley

54 God Cupid, oh fie, oh fie, oh fie!
    God Cupid, oh fie, oh fie!
        I am vexed full sore —
        Oh, thou son of a whore,
    Take pity on me or I die, I die,
    Take pity on me or I die!
        My face is pale and wan,
        My blood is turned to a jelly;
        In my heart I have a great pain —
        Oh, oh, how I long for a man!
        With a sol my fa la long tre down derry.

Thomas Duffett

55 A young man lately in our town
    He went to bed one night,

He had no sooner laid him down
But was troubled with a sprite:
So vigorously the spirit stood,
Let him do what he can,
      Oh then he said,
       'It must be laid
By a woman, not a man.'

A handsome maid did undertake
And into th' bed she leapt,
And to allay the spirit's power
Full close to him she crept;
She, having such a guardian care
Her office to discharge,
She opened wide her conjuring-book
And laid her leaves at large.

Her office she did well perform
Within a little space,
Then up she rose and down he lay
And durst not show his face.
She took her leave and away she went,
When she had done the deed,
Saying, 'If 't chance to come again,
Then send for me with speed.'

New Academy of Compliments, 1671

56 As Oyster Nell stood by her tub,
     To show her vicious inclination
She gave her noblest parts a scrub
     And sighed for want of copulation.
A vintner of no little fame,
     Who excellent red and white can sell ye
Beheld the little, dirty dame
     As she stood scratching of her belly.

'Come in,' says he, 'you silly slut,
   'Tis now a rare convenient minute;
I'll lay the itching of your scut,
   Except some greedy devil be in it!'
With that the flat-capped fubsy smiled
   And would have blushed, but that she could not.
'Alas,' says she, 'we're soon beguiled
   By men to do those things we should not.'

From door they went behind the bar,
   As is by common fame reported,
And there upon a Turkey chair
   Unseen the loving couple sported;
But being called by company
   As he was taking pains to please her,
'I'm coming, coming, sir!' says he.
   'My dear, and so am I!' says she, sir.

Her mole-hill belly swelled about
   Into a mountain quickly after,
And when the pretty mouse crept out,
   The creature caused a mighty laughter;
And now she has learnt the pleasing game,
   Although much pain and shame it cost her,
She daily ventures at the same
   And shuts and opens like an oyster.

Penkethman's Jests, 1721

57 *Nanny*   I'm near fifteen and I have not seen
             A man that I like, where e'er I have been:
             The finikin tailor who makes his address
             Is a lousy young coxcomb, I needs must
                                          confess,
             And take away bodkin, his threads and his
                                          goose,

All the rest of his tools are scarce worth a
louse.

Jenny   And there is my butcher, a bloody young
knave,
A pretty spruce lass he gladly would have,
With his tool at his arse and a dainty blue
frock,
And impudent language he has a great stock.
He often comes to me, but 'Foh!' out I cry,
'No butcherly booby with Jenny shall lie!'

Nanny   And I have a baker that busses me oft;
His teeth are like ivory, his lips they are soft,
But he stinks of sweat as bad as a jakes —
Oh, that he smelt but so sweet as his cakes!
I' faith I could love him exceedingly well,
But his wife, I believe, may as well live in
hell.

Jenny   No, no, let us live, and live in man's spite:
From all that fond sex I'll ever take flight,
Unless a blind usurer courts me with gold,
No mortal shall ever touch my copyhold.
A pox upon all their dissembling tricks!
They'll lie from sixteen to sixty and six.

New London Drollery, 1687

58 *Quaker*   Now Mary, now tell me
What hurt is in this?
If you deal with the wicked
I yield 'tis amiss;
But the Saints with each other
May tumble and kiss,
And we'll raise up our spirits again.

59

Maid   Well, Master, I yield
         Your refreshings were good,
   And since your impulses
       I have not withstood,
   You'll give me, I know,
       What you promised you would
And we'll raise up our spirits again.

Quaker   Yea, damosel, my kindness
        Shall never decay,
   But let not thy apparel
      Be gaudy and gay.
   Here's thirty good shillings —
      Come buss and away,
Now we've raised up our spirits again.

The Secret Sinners, c. 1686

59 Captain   Now boys, our voyage is out
   And we are richly fraught:
      While fools do stay
      At home and play
   We trace the world about.

Pilot   Would I were in close harbour,
   From noise of Port and Larbor!

Boatswain   Thou'dst run ahead
      With Jenny in bed
   And anchor in her harbour.

Pilot   But if she should not come to it,
   If she should not come to it?

Boatswain   If she has a rudder
      As well as her mother,
   I'll warrant thee, boy, she will do it.

Sixteen fathom and a quarter, Master.
                              Port.

Captain   Haul in your main braces, down with your
              anchor, and lore your topsail to the Royal
              Sovereign of London.

                              Matthew Taubman

60 *Enter a country lass with a rake, as at haymaking.*
    Oh, why thus alone must I pass the long day?
    Were a gentleman by 'twere sweet to make hay,
    And on the grass coupled and jig it away.
    I'll then go sell all, ev'n my rake and my pail,
    To buy me a high topping and hugeous long tail:
    Your powdered wild boars will then all come to
                              woo;
    I'll learn how to slant it and quickly come to,
    And serve a town husband as other wives do.

    I hate a dull clown who knows hardly what's what,
    Who shruggling and grinning stands twirling his hat,
    Nor dares tell a body what he would be at;
    With smoke and worse liquor he sots and he feasts
    And instead of his mistress he fondles his beasts;
    With his hands in his pockets he whistling goes by
    Or by me on a haycock he snoring does lie,
    When the booby much better himself might employ.

    Enter a town spark.
    'Tis sultry weather, pretty maid.
    Come, let's retire to yonder shade.

                              Peter Motteux

61 Have you any work for the sow-gelder, ho?
    My horn goes too high, too low.

Have you any pigs, calves or colts?
Have you any lambs in your holts
To cut for the stone?
Here comes a cunning one.

Have you any brauches to spade
Or e'er a fair maid
That would be a nun?
Come kiss me, 'tis done.
Hark how my merry horn doth blow
Too high, too low. Too high, too low.

New Academy of Compliments, 1671

62 'Oh, Anis,' quoth he. 'Well, Thomas,' quoth she,
'What wouldst thou say, man, unto me?'
'I love thee,' quoth he. 'Dost love me?' quoth she.
'Oh, I'm the more beholding to thee.'
'To bed then,' quoth he. 'No, Thomas,' quoth she,
'Not till the parson hath said all unto me.'
'I'z bump thee,' quoth he. 'Wou't bump me?' quoth she.
'Oh, I'm the more beholding to thee.'
'How lik'st it?' quoth he. 'Well, Thomas,' quoth she,
'So thou com'st but once more unto me.'
'That I will,' quoth he. 'Sayst thou so?' quoth she.
'Oh, I'm the more beholding to thee.'

New Academy of Compliments, 1671

63 'Now the weather is warm, let us laugh and be merry.
My Betty, let us walk and taste of a cherry.
Then be not affrighted, for thus we will do:
Thou shalt have my cherry, and cherry-stones, too.'

'Then use me not roughly, but prithee be kind;
I thought to such tricks you had not been inclined;

But since thou to me thy mind dost declare,
We'll walk to the place where the cherry-trees are.'

No sooner they came to sit under the boughs
But Betty she taxed him with breaking of vows.
Quoth Johnny, 'Don't say so, my love it is true:
Thou shalt have my cherry, and cherry-stones too.

And this is a vow I am resolved to keep,
For a maidenhead I will have ere I do sleep.'
As soon as she heard him she quickly was won,
And under the cherry-tree there it was done.

Says Betty, 'Oh, will not these cherries prove ill
And be the cause for my belly to swell?
As many young maidens has cause for to rue,
For eating of cherries, and cherry-stones too.'

Some lads and some lasses they walked so near,
This gallant young couple they did overhear,
And came to behold them, which when they did see
They were all agog at the same sport to be.

Under the green trees each lad took his lass
And laid them down softly upon the green grass;
Such work there was done the like never was known,
Whilst Robin kissed Margaret, Thomas kissed Joan.

What followed those joys you may easily guess,
For their bellies did swell, as they after confess,
Which brought their disgrace and quickly was known,
For each lass had a child, but husband none.

Such sighing and moaning that there was then,
For they said they would never love cherries again;
The cherries they liked, but the stones did not please,
For it made their bellies to swell by degrees.

You maidens of Kent, take warning by this
And be not so forward to hug and to kiss,
Which are the forerunners of mischief indeed,
And for our past follies our hearts now doth bleed.

For one minute's pleasure must we pay so dear?
What is done in secret so plain must appear;
For I can't get a husband, do all what I can,
And my heart it will break for want of a man.

Wit's Cabinet, circa 1700

64 The old wife she sent to the miller her daughter,
To grind her grist quickly and so return back;
The miller so worked it that in eight months after
Her belly was filled as full as her sack:
        Young Robin so pleased her
        That when she came home
She gaped like a stuck pig and stared like a mome;
She hoydened, she scampered, she hollowed and
                        whooped,
        And all the day long
        This, this was her song:
'Hoy, was ever maiden so lerricom pooped?'

'Oh, Nelly,' cried Celie, 'thy clothes are all mealy;
Both backside and belly are rumpled all o'er;
You mope now and slubber — why, what a pox ail ye?
I'll go to the miller and know all, ye whore.'
        She went, and the miller
        So grinding did ply
She came cutting capers a foot and half high;
She waddled and straddled and hollowed and whooped,
        And all the day long
        This, this was her song:
'Hoy, were ever two sisters so lerricom pooped?'

Then Mary o'th'Dairy, a third of the number,
Would fain know the cause they so jigged it about.
The miller her wishes long would not encumber,
But in the old manner the secret made out:
   Thus Celie and Nelly
   And Mary the mild
Were just about harvest-time all big with child;
They danced in a hay and they hollowed and
          whooped,
   And all the day long
   This was their song:
'Hoy, were ever three sisters so lerricom pooped?'

And when they were big they did stare on each other,
And crying, 'Oh, sisters, what shall we now do?
For all our young bantlings we have but one father,
And they in one month will all come to town too.
   Oh, why did we run
   In such haste to the mill,
To Robin, who always the toll-dish would fill?
He bumped up our bellies, then hollowed and
          whooped,'
   And all the day long
   This, this was their song:
'Hoy, were ever three sisters so lerricom pooped?'

Wit and Mirth: or,
Pills to Purge Melancholy,
1699 – 1700

65 There was a fair maiden came out of Kent;
To be kissed by a joiner was her intent,
To be kissed by a joiner was her intent.

'I have a job of work for you to do,

65

To make me a bed go jig a jog goo,
To make my bed go jig a jog goo.'

'And when would you have this job of work done?'
'By the faith of my body, soon as you can,
By the faith of my body, soon as you can.'

When this job of work it was thoroughly done,
Then he laid this fair maiden thereupon,
Then he laid this fair maiden thereupon.

He knocked in a pin where a pin should be,
Which made the bed to go jig a joggee,
Which made the bed to go jig a joggee.

But in the old mother came full of woe,
With 'Oh, fie, daughter, why would you do so?'
With 'Oh, fie, daughter, why would you do so?'

'Since it must be done, mother, why not he
That would make my bed go jig a joggee?
That would make my bed go jig a joggee?'

New Academy of Compliments, 1671

66 'I'd have you,' quoth he.
    'Would you have me?' quoth she.
        'Oh, where, sir?'

    'In my chamber,' quoth he.
    'In your chamber?' quoth she.
        'Why there, sir?'

    'To kiss you,' quoth he.
    'To kiss me?' quoth she.
        'Oh, why, sir?'

    'Cause I love it,' quoth he.

66

'Do you love it?' quoth she.
'So do I, sir.'

Windsor Drollery, 1672

III

Olinda   Let me see Elysium quickly, and tell me truly what they do there.

Conjuror Madam, it is so little, and so like what's done in this world, that it is not worth your knowing; but since you command, I must obey. Let idle poets speak their fancies of Elysium, but I that have been there must speak the truth; in short, madam, all the women do nothing else but sing, 'John, come kiss me now,' and then the men give 'em a green gown upon the flowery banks, and there they commit love together.

Olinda   Do they not dance in Elysium?

Conjuror Yes, madam, as you shall see.

THE DUMB LADY

67 Man, man, man is for the woman made
    And the woman made for man;
    As the spur is for the jade,
    As the scabbard for the blade,
    As for digging is the spade,
    As for liquor is the can,
 So man, man, man is for the woman made
    And the woman made for man.

    As the sceptre's to be swayed,
    As for night's the serenade,
    As for pudding is the pan,
    And to cool you is the fan,
 So man, man, man is for the woman made
    And the woman made for man.

    Be she widow, wife or maid,
    Be she wanton, be she staid,
    Be she well or ill arrayed,
    Whore, bawd or harridan,
 Yet man, man, man is for the woman made
    And the woman made for man.

Penkethman's Jests, 1721

68 Let's love and drink and drink and love and drink on.
 What have we else in this dull world to think on
 But still to love, to drink and love and drink on?

 Let's love and drink and drink and love for ever,
 And let each nymph be made a kind believer;
 For he that loves and drinks will ne'er deceive her.

Thomas Duffett

69 It is not, Celia, in our power
    To say how long our love will last;

It may be we within this hour
May lose those joys we now do taste.
The Blessed, that immortal be,
From change in love are only free.

Then since we mortal lovers are
Ask not how long our love will last;
But while it does let us take care
Each minute be with pleasure passed.
Were it not madness to deny
To live, because we are sure to die?

Sir George Etherege

70 Ancient person, for whom I
All the flattering youth defy,
Long be it ere thou grow old,
Aching, shaking, crazy, cold;
    But still continue as thou art,
    Ancient person of my heart.

On thy withered lips and dry,
Which like barren furrows lie,
Brooding kisses I will pour
Shall thy youthful [heat] restore
(Such kind showers in autumn fall,
And a second spring recall);
    Nor from thee will ever part,
    Ancient person of my heart.

Thy nobler part, which but to name
In our sex would be counted shame,
By age's frozen grasp possessed,
From [his] ice shall be released,
And soothed by my reviving hand,
In former warmth and vigour stand.

All a lover's wish can reach
For thy joy my love shall teach,
And for thy pleasure shall improve
All that art can add to love.
   Yet still I love thee without art,
   Ancient person of my heart.

John Wilmot, Earl of Rochester

71 A monarch I'll be when I lie by thy side,
   And thy pretty hand my sceptre shall guide.

Wit's Cabinet, circa 1700

72 To charming Celia's arms I flew
      And there all night I feasted;
   No god such transport ever knew
      Or mortal ever tasted.
   Left in the sweet, tumultuous joys
      And blessed beyond expressing,
   'How can your slave, my fair,' said I,
      'Reward so great a blessing?
   The whole creation's wealth survey,
      O'er both the Indies wander,
   Ask what bribed senates give away
      Or fighting monarchs squander;
   The richest spoils of earth and air,
      The rifled ocean's treasure,
   'Tis all too poor a bribe by far,
      To purchase so much pleasure.'
   She blushing cried, 'My life, my dear,
      Since Celia thus you fancy,
   Give her, but 'tis too much, I fear,
      A rundlet of right Nantzy.'

Wit's Cabinet, circa 1700

73 Whilst Alexis lay pressed
    In her arms he loved best,
    With his hands round her neck
    And his head on her breast,
    He found the fierce pleasure too hasty to stay
    And his soul in the tempest just flying away.

    When Celia saw this,
    With a sigh and a kiss,
    She cried, 'Oh, my dear, I am robbed of my bliss.
    'Tis unkind to your love and unfaithfully done
    To leave me behind you and die all alone.'

    The youth, though in haste
    And breathing his last,
    In pity died slowly, while she died more fast,
    Till at length she cried, 'Now, my dear, now let us go.
    Now die, my Alexis, and I will die too.'

    Thus entranced they did lie
    Till Alexis did try
    To recover new breath, that again he might die.
    Then often they died; but the more they did so
    The nymph died more quick and the shepherd more
                                             slow.
                                        John Dryden

74 She lay all naked in her bed
        And I myself lay by;
    No veil nor curtain there was spread,
        No covering but I.
    Her head upon one shoulder seeks
        To hang in careless wise;
    All full of blushes were her cheeks
        And wishes were her eyes.

Her blood lay flushing in her face,
    As on a message came
To say that in some other place
    It meant some other game;
Her nether lip, moist, plump and fair,
    Millions of kisses crowned,
Which ripe and uncropped dangled there
    And weighed the branches down.

Her breasts, that lay swelled full and high,
    Bred pleasant pangs in me
And all the world I did defy
    For that felicity;
Her thighs and belly, soft and plump,
    To me were only shown:
To have seen such meat and not to eat
    Would have angered anyone.

Her knees lay up, but stoutly bent,
    And all was hollow under,
As if on easy terms they meant
    To fall unforced asunder;
Just so the Cyprian Queen did lie
    Expecting in her bower,
When too long stay had kept the boy
    Beyond his promised hour.

'Dull clown,' quoth she, 'why dost delay
    Such proffered bliss to take?
Canst thou find no other way
    Similitudes to make?'
Mad with delight, I thundered in
    And threw mine arms about her,
But a pox upon't, 'twas but a dream,
    And so I lay without her.

Merry Drollery Complete, 169

75 Her lips are two brimmers of claret,
      Where first I began to miscarry;
              Her breasts of delight
              Are two bottles of white
      And her eyes are two cups of canary.

Sir Charles Sedley

76 How wanton and frolic's this age,
      Wherein gallants so briskly invade
  The misses that furnish the stage
      And the madams in masquerade!

Unseen and unknown they still court
      And walk a corant to and fro;
Bad faces ne'er hinder the sport
      If the blade's well provided below.

The ladies make choice by the size,
      The gallants by garb and proportion,
And when their brisk spirits do rise
      They fall to their carnal devotion.

There needs neither parents' consent,
      A jointure nor rites of the Church:
If fiercely the gallant be bent,
      The ladies scarce leave him i' th' lurch.

Yet if he too faintly pursue
      The idol he seems to adore,
With a frisk she'll bid him adieu
      And leave the young fop at the door.

Thomas Rawlins

77 I love somebody, I love nobody,
     Somebody, nobody dearly:

I love somebody, I love nobody,
Somebody, nobody dearly.
Be she black or be she brown,
She's the best in all the town,
So she keep her belly down,
Down, down, down, down:
There's no fault to be found,
So she keep her belly down.

Thomas Shadwell

78 Awake, pretty shepherdess,
    Hark! the birds sing.
Arise, my best love,
    See, the violets they spring;
Each smiles for to see
    That herself is so fair
And that the cold winter
    That made her so bare
Is vanished and gone.
    Let's give place to flight,
Let us love all the day
    And let's revel all night;
Let envy and jealousies
    Never disturb us;
To no fear let's give place
    That has power to curb us.

Love's Masterpiece, 1683

79 In a room for delight, the landskip of love,
    Like a shady old lawn,
    With the curtains half-drawn,
My love and I lay in the cool of the day
    Till our joys did remove.

So fierce was our fight and so smart every stroke
That Love, the little scout,
Was put to the rout;
His bow was unbent, every arrow was spent
And his quiver all broke.

Nathaniel Lee

80 Last night I dreamed of my love
When sleep did overtake her.
It was a pretty, drowsy rogue;
She slept; I durst not wake her.

Her lips were like to coral red;
A thousand times I kissed 'um,
And a thousand more I might have stol'n,
For she had ne'er a miss'd 'um.

Her crisped locks, like threads of gold,
Hung dangling o'er the pillow;
Great pity 'twas that one so fair
Should wear the rainbow-willow.

I folded down the holland sheet
A little below her belly,
But what I did you ne'er shall know,
Nor is it meet to tell ye.

Her belly's like to yonder hill —
Some call it Mount of Pleasure —
And underneath there springs a well
Which no man's depth can measure.

New Academy of Compliments, 1671

81 Hey boy, hey boy,
Come, come away boy,

77

And bring me my longing desire:
A lass that is neat and can well do the feat
When lusty young blood is on fire.

Let her body be tall
And her waist be small,
And her age not above eighteen;
Let her care for no bed, but here let her spread
Her mantle upon the green.

Let her face be fair
And her breasts be bare,
And a voice let her have that can warble;
Let her belly be soft, but to mount me aloft
Let her bounding buttocks be marble.

Let her have a cherry lip
Where I nectar may sip;
Let her eyes be as black as the sloe.
Dangling locks I do love, so that those hung above
Are the same with what grows below.

Oh, such a bonny lass
May bring wonders to pass
And make me grow younger and younger;
And whene'er we do part she'll be mad at the heart
That I am able to tarry no longer.

Wit and Mirth: or,
Pills to Purge Melancholy,
1699 — 1700

82 In a cottage by the mountain
Lives a very pretty maid,
Who lay sleeping by a fountain
Underneath a myrtle shade;

Her petticoat of wanton sarcenet
The amorous wind about did move
And quite unveiled
And quite unveiled the Throne of Love
And quite unveiled the Throne of Love.

Aphra Behn

83 A gentleman, seeing a very pretty maid with her
valentine pinned on her sleeve, intending to play
the wag with her, asked if her waistcoat was to
be let. 'Yes, sir,' said she. 'To be let alone.' 'I am
content,' said he, 'to let your waistcoat alone, but
not your petticoat.'

Nugae Venales, 1686

84   Buff's a fine sport,
          And so's course o' park;
          But both come short
          Of a dance in the dark.
            We trip it completely,
            The pipe sounds so neatly,
            But that which surpasses
            Is the breath of the lasses.
          Oh, the pretty rogues kiss featly!

Robert Stapylton

85 Jogging on from yonder's green,
Oh, the pleasant'st sight I've seen:
John and Dolly jog, jog, jogging,
John and Dolly jogging on.
Themselves cooling, John was fooling,
Cried she, 'Will you ne'er have done
Jog, jog, jog, jog, jog, jog, jogging on?

The sun shines, make hay,
Make hay, make hay, make hay, dear John!'
    Hey ho, hey ho, that I might do so,
    Jog, jog, jog, jog, jogging
    Jog, jog, jog, jogging on.

John, to ease her of her pain,
Ended and begun again;
He grew weary, jog, jog, jogging,
She more cheery, jogging on,
Cried, 'My deary, prithee tarry,
Sure you han't already done
Jog, jog, jog, jog, jog, jog, jogging on?
The sun's down, pray stay,
Pray stay, pray stay, good John!'
    Hey ho, that I might do so,
    Jog, jog, jogging on.

                     Penkethman's Jests, 1721

86 There were two bumpkins loved a lass
    And striving who should have her;
She presumed of what she had
    And they of what they gave her.
Hey ho, hey ho, my heart's delight,
    Carouse away all sorrow —
Let me tickle the wench twice tonight
    And she shall be thine tomorrow.

But we were both of one consent
    And something had some savour,
And let a poor man be content
    With half a wench's favour.
Hey ho, etc.

But this is still against all sense,

Which ever more has vexed us,
That every lobcock has his wench
   And we but one betwixt us.
Hey ho, etc.

Good brother, let us not dismay,
   What hap so e'er betide us,
For fear a third should come this way
   And pull our wench beside us.
Hey ho, etc.

For women they are winning things,
   As mutable as may be;
No bird that ever flew with wings
   So subtle is as they be.
Hey ho, etc.

No matter who shall pledge her first:
   Affections are but blindness;
And let the world say what they list,
   We'll take her double kindness.
Hey ho, etc.

For she has granted both our suits,
   When we came first unto her,
And he shall ride in both our boots
   That comes the next to woo her.
Hey ho, etc.

                        Penkethman's Jests, 1721

87 Have y' any cracked maidenheads to new leach or
                                   mend?
   Have y' any old maidenheads to fell or to change?
   Bring 'em to me — with a little pretty gin
   I'll clout 'em, I'll mend 'em, I'll knock in a pin

Shall make 'em as good maids again
As ever they have been.

Windsor Drollery, 1672

88 Now wanton lads and lasses do make hay,
Which unto lewd temptations makes great way
With tumbling on the cocks, which acted duly
Doth cause much mischief in the month of July.

Poor Robin's Almanack, 1687

89 Johnny took Joan by the arm
And led her unto the haycock;
And yet he did her no harm,
Although he felt under her smock.
        Although he did touse her,
        Although he did rouse her
Until she backwards did fall,
        She did not complain
        Nor his kindness refrain,
But prayed him to put it in all.

Love's Masterpiece, 1683

90 Poor Jenny and I we toiled
A long, long summer's day
Till we were almost spoiled
With making of the hay.
Her kerchief was of holland clear
Bound low upon her brow;
I'se whispered something in her ear,
But what's that to you?

Her stockings were of kersey green,
Well stitched with yellow silk.
Oh, sike a leg was never seen,

Her skin as white as milk;
Her hair as black as any crow,
And sweet her mouth was too.
Oh, Jenny daintily could mow,
But what's that to you?

Her petticoats were not so low
As ladies now do wear 'em;
She needed not a page, I trow,
For I was by to bear 'em;
I'z took 'em up all in my hand
And I think her linen too,
Which made a friend of mine to stand,
But what's that to you?

King Solomon had wives enough
And concubines a number;
Yet I'z possess more happiness
And he had more of cumber.
My joy surmounts a wedded life;
With fear she lets me mow;
A wench is better than a wife,
But what's that to you?

The lily and the rose combine
To make my Jenny fair;
There's no contentment sike as mine,
I'm almost void of care.
But yet I fear my Jenny's face
Will cause more men to woo,
Which I shall take for a disgrace
But what's that to you?

New Academy of Compliments,
1671

91 Now country Tom and Tib have their desire '
   And roll and tumble freely on the grass;
   The milkmaid gets a green gown for her hire
   And all in sport the time away do pass:
       They sing, they frisk, they clip, they roll and kiss,
       Still making pleasant use of time as 'tis.

Poor Robin, A Prognostication, 1675

92 No youth here need willow wear,
   No beauteous maid will her lover destroy;
   The gentle little lass will yield
   In the soft daisy field:
       Freely our pleasures we here enjoy.
   No great Juno we boldly defy,
   With young Chloris' cheeks or fair Celia's eye:
   We let all those things alone and enjoy our own,
   Every night with our beauties lie.

Broadside, circa 1685

93 *Q* Who is a bashful woman?
   A She who, lying on her back, covers her face with
       her smock.
   Q Who is a fearful woman?
   A She who claps her tail between her legs or she who
       dares not sleep without a man.
   Q Who is a bold, daring woman?
   A She that dares singly oppose ten men at the en-
       trance of one breach.
   Q What is a curious woman?
   A One who desires to know what every man can do.
   Q Who are most gluttonous?
   A Women; for having two mouths — one for the day
       and the other for the night — they feed conti-
       nually.

84

Q A maid, being asked whether she would choose to be changed into a hen or a goose?

A Her answer was, 'Into a hen'; and the reason was, because the hen enjoys her cock all the year round, but the goose only in springtime.

Nugae Venales, 1686

94   Young wenches have a wanton sport . . . they get upon a table-board and then gather up their knees and their coats with their hands as high as they can, and then they wobble to and fro with their buttocks, as if they were kneading of dough with their arses, and say these words . . .

> My dame is sick and gone to bed
> And we'll go mould some cockle-bread;
> Up with my heels and down with my head,
> And this is the way to mould cockle-bread.

John Aubrey

95 My lady and her maid, upon a merry pin,
They made a match at farting, who should the wager
                win.
Joan lights three candles then and sets them bolt
                upright;
With the first fart she blew them out,
With the next she gave them light,
In comes my lady then, with all her might and main,
And blew them out, and in and out, and out and in
                again.

An Antidote against Melancholy, 1661

Mrs Crossbite	Have you ravished my daughter, then, you old goat? ravished my daughter! — ravished my daughter! speak villain.
Gripe	By yea and by nay, no such matter.
Mrs Crossbite	A canting rogue, too! Take notice, landlord, he has ravished my daughter, you see her all in tears and distraction; and see there the wicked engine of the filthy execution. —

LOVE IN A WOOD

96 Fair Chloris in a pigsty lay;
     Her tender herd lay by her.
  She slept; in murmuring gruntlings they,
  Complaining of the scorching day,
     Her slumbers thus inspire.

  She dreamt whilst she with careful pains
     Her snowy arms employed
  In ivory pails to fill out grains,
  One of her love-convicted swains
     Thus hasting to her cried:

  'Fly, nymph! Oh, fly ere 'tis too late
     A dear, loved life to save;
  Rescue your bosom pig from fate
  Who now expires, hung in the gate
     That leads to Flora's cave.

  Myself had tried to set him free
     Rather than brought the news,
  But I am so abhorred by thee
  That ev'n thy darling's life from me
     I know thou wouldst refuse.'

  Struck with the news, as quick she flies
     As blushes to her face;
  Not the bright lightning from the skies,
  Nor love, shot from her brighter eyes,
     Move half so swift a pace.

  This plot, it seems, the lustful slave
     Had laid against her honour,
  Which not one god took care to save,
  For he pursues her to the cave
     And throws himself upon her.

Now piercèd is her virgin zone;
  She feels the foe within it,
She hears a broken amorous groan,
The panting lover's fainting moan,
  Just in the happy minute.

Frighted she wakes, and waking frigs.
  Nature thus kindly eased
In dreams raised by her murmuring pigs
And her own thumb between her legs,
  She's innocent and pleased.

John Wilmot, Earl of Rochester

97 How happy and free is the plunder
When we care not for Jove and his thunder:
    Having entered a town,
    The lasses go down
And to their o'er comers lie under.
  Why then should we study to love and look pale
  And make long addresses to what will grow stale?

If her fingers be soft, long and slender,
When once we have made her to render
    She will handle a flute
    Better far than a lute
And make what was hard to grow tender.
  Then why should we study to love and look pale
  And make long addresses to what will grow stale?

If her hair of the delicate brown is
And her belly as soft as the down is,
    She will fire your heart,
    In performing her part,
With a flame that more hot than the town is.

> *Why then should we study to love and look pale*
> *And make long addresses to what will grow stale?*

When the houses with flashes do glitter
Who can sever our sweet from the bitter?
  And in that bright night
  We can take our delight:
No damsel shall 'scape but we'll hit her.
> *Why then should we study to love and look pale*
> *And make long addresses, but never prevail?*

       New Academy of Compliments, 1671

98 As on a purple quilt I chose
  By night to take my sweet repose,
  When dewy sleep fell on my breast
  And all my cares lay calmed in rest,
  My wanton fancy sporting lay
  And called my roving thoughts to play,
  Who in their sport and am'rous flight
  Made up this landskip of delight.
  Methoughts (but oh, 'twas but a dream)
  I wandering spied a spotless train
  Of beauteous virgins, where each face
  Provoked enough to the amorous chase.
  Straight the coy phantoms fled away,
  Nor would for my kind courtship stay;
  I followed straight, but, lo, hard by
  A troop of gallant youths did lie,
  Who there would fain have rivalled me
  And forced me back with raillery.
  Yet this, alas, but fanned the fire
  And added wings to my desire:
  Methought I made the greater haste
  And seized the amorous prey at last;
  And then I proffered at a kiss,

But waked in the interim of bliss.
Curse on my eyes, that opened day
And chased those pleasant forms away!
My eyes, that now will useless be,
If I such sights may sleeping see.
Thus raving I lay down, and then
I only wished to dream again.

Anacreon Done into English, 1683

99 Near famous Covent Garden
    A dome there stands on high
    With a fa, la, la, la &c.

Where kings are represented
    And queens in metre die
    With a fa, la, la, la &c.

The beaus and men of business
    Diversions hither bring,
To hear the wanton doxies prate
    And see 'em dance and sing
    With a fa, la, la, la &c.

Here Phillis is a darling,
    As she herself gives out,
    For a fa, la, la, la &c.

As tight a lass as ever
    Did use a double clout
    On her fa, la, la, la &c.

She's brisk and gay and cunning
    And wants a wedlock yoke;
Her mother was before her
    As good as ever strook
    For a fa, la, la, la &c.

Young suitors she had many
   From squire up to lord
      For a fa, la, la, la &c.

And daily she refused 'em,
   For virtue was the word
      With her fa, la, la, la &c.

A saint she would be thought
   And dissembled all she could,
But jolly rakes all knew she was
   Of playhouse flesh and blood
      And her fa, la, la, la &c.

Her mother when encouraged
   With warm Geneva dose
      And a fa, la, la, la &c.

Still cried, 'Take care, dear Philly,
   To keep thy haunches close,
      And this fa, la, la, la &c.'

This made her stand out stoutly
   Opposing all that come,
Though twenty demi-cannon
   Still were mounted at her bum
      And her fa, la, la, la &c.

The knight and country squire
   Were shot with her disdain
      And her fa, la, la, la &c.

The lawyer was outwitted,
   The hardy soldier slain
      By her fa, la, la, la &c.

The bluff tarpaulin sailor

In vain cried 'Hard a port!'
She baffled sharks at sea
    As the country, town and court
        With her fa, la, la, la &c.

The God of Love, grown angry
    That Phillis seemed so shy
        Of her fa, la, la, la &c.

Resolved her pride to humble
    And rout her pish and fie;
        And her fa, la, la, la &c.

He sent a splayfoot tailor,
    Who knew well how to stitch
And in a little time had found
    A button for her britch
        And her fa, la, la, la &c.

Yet was it not so close,
    But 'tis known, without all doubt,
        With a fa, la, la, la &c.

A little human figure
    Has secretly dropped out
        From her fa, la, la, la &c.

And though some pretty scandal
    Pursue this venial fact,
Her mother she swears Soons and C —
    Her honour is intact
        And her fa, la, la, la &c.

Oh Phillis, then be wise
    And give ease to lovers racked
        For your fa, la, la, la &c.

Let coyness be abated;
　　You know the pitcher's cracked
　　　　By a fa, la, la, la &c.

For shame! let lousy tailors
　　No more your love trepan,
Since nine of 'em, you know 'tis said,
　　Can hardly make a man
　　　　With a fa, la, la, la &c.

Penkethman's Jests, 1721

100　Phillis, the fairest of Love's foes,
　　　But fiercer than a dragon,
　　　Phillis who scorned the powdered beaux,
　　　Her arse had scarce a rag on.

　　　Compelled by want, the wretched maid
　　　Did sad complaints begin,
　　　Which surly Strephon hearing said
　　　It were both shame and sin
　　　To pity a proud, lazy jade
　　　Who'd neither fuck nor spin.

Harleian MS. 6914

101　I told young Jenny I loved her
　　　With a zeal that I thought would have moved her;
　　　I gave her earnest in hand to boot,
　　　For I knew by my bargain that I could stand to 't;
　　　But the gypsy, cunningly taught by her sire,
　　　　　Cried, 'Marry or else forsake me.
　　　When you've filled my belly and your desire,
　　　　　You'll be hanged before you will take me.'

　　　While her Dad of his own accord, sir,
　　　Made himself as drunk as a lord, sir,

In hopes t' have found it a wedding day,
I took up my Jenny and carr'd her away.
Let her scratch and bite, let her kick and wince,
    Now I've got her into my clutches;
She's witty and fair, she's a gem for a prince
    And in time she may be a duchess.

Wit at a Venture, 1674

102   A foolish wench, merely out of revenge, complained
to a justice that such a man would have ravished her.
'What did he do?' says he. 'He tied my hands so fast I
could not stir them.' 'And what else?' 'Why, sir,' said
she, 'he would have tied my legs, too, but I had the
wit to keep them far enough asunder!'

Nugae Venales, 1686

103 *Enter Alberto pulling in Flora and singing:*

He took her about the middle so small
And threw her upon the ground.

Flora   If you have any more of that song I'll
turn you out of the door again; you will
never leave this ribaldry, you are in a
sweet pickle.

Flora's Vagaries, 1670

104   A young, buxom baggage with a candle in her hand
was set upon by a hotspur who by all means must have
a bout with her; but she vowed if he meddled with
her she would burn him. 'Will you?' says he. 'I'll try
that.' And thereupon he blew out the candle, thinking
himself safe from the threat. However, not long after
he found she was as good as her word.

Nugae Venales, 1686

105 The four and twentieth day of May —
         Of all days in the year —
     A virgin lady, fresh and gay,
         Did privately appear:
     Hard by a river side got she
         And did sing loud the rather,
     'Cause she was sure she was secure
         And had an intent to bath her.

     With glittering, glancing, jealous eyes
         She slily looks about,
     To see if any lurking spies
         Were hid to find her out,
     And being well resolved that none
         Could see her nakedness,
     She pulled her robes off one by one
         And did herself undress.

     Her purple mantle, fringed with gold,
         Her ivory hands unpinned;
     It would have made a coward bold
         Or tempted a saint to 'a sinned.
     She turned about and looked around.
         Quoth she, 'I hope I'm safe';
     Then her rosy petticoat
         She presently put off.

     The snow-white smock which she had on,
         Transparently to deck her,
     Looked like cambric or lawn
         Upon an alabaster picture,
     Through which array I did faintly spy
         Her belly and her back;
     Her limbs were straight and all was white
         But that which should be black.

Into a fluent stream she leapt,
    She looked like Venus' glass,
The fishes from all quarters crept
    To see what angel 'twas;
She did so like a vision look
    Or fairy in a dream
'Twas thought the sun the skies forsook
    And dropped into the stream.

Each fish did wish himself a man —
    About her all was drawn —
And at the sight of her began
    To spread abroad their spawn.
She turned to swim upon her back;
    And so displayed her banner;
If Jove had then in Heaven been
    He would have dropped upon her.

A lad that long her love had been
    And could obtain no grace
For all her prying lay unseen,
    Hid in a secret place,
Who had often been repulsed
    When he did come to woo her,
Pulled off his clothes and furiously
    Did run and leap in to her.

She squeaked, she cried, and down she dived;
    He brought her up again;
He brought her o'er upon the shore
    And then — and then — and then —
As Adam did old Eve enjoy,
    You may guess what I mean;
Because she all uncovered lay
    He covered her again.

With watered eyes she pants and cries,
   'I'm utterly undone,
If you will not be wed to me
   Ere the next morning sun.'
He answered her he ne'er would stir
   Out of her sight till then:
'We'll both clap hands in wedlock's bands,
   Marry, and to 't again'.

Wit and Mirth: or,
Pills to Purge Melancholy,
1699 — 1700

106 'Twas when summer was rosy,
   In woods and fields many a posy,
When late young flaxen-haired Nelly
   Was waylaid by bonny black Willy:
He ogled her and teased her,
   He smuggled her and squeezed her,
He grabbled her, too, very near the belly.
   She cried, 'I never will hear ye.
Oh, Lord! oh, Lord! I can't bear ye.
   Ye tickle, tickle so, tickle, tickle so, Willy.'

Soon the fit, though, was over
   And Nelly her breath did recover,
When Willy bated his wooing
   And coolly prepared to be going,
When Nelly, though he teased her
   And grabbled her and squeezed her,
Cried, 'Stay a little. I vow and swear I could kill ye.
   Another touch I can bear ye.
Oh, Lord! oh, Lord! I will hear ye,
   Then tickle me again, tickle me again, Willy!'

Wit and Mirth: or, Pills to
*Purge Melancholy,*1699 — 1700

107 The sun was just setting, the reaping was done,
  And over the common I tripped it alone;
  Then whom should I meet but young Dick of our town,
  Who swore ere I went I should have a green gown.
      He pressed me, I stumbled,
      He pushed me, I tumbled,
      He kissed me, I grumbled,
      But still he kissed on.
  If he be not hampered for serving me so,
      May I be worse rumpled
      Worse tumbled and jumbled
      Where'er, where'er I go.

  Before an old justice I summoned the spark,
  And how d'ye think I was served by his clerk?
  He pulled out his inkhorn and asked me his fee:
  'You now shall relate the whole business,' quoth he.
      He pressed me &c.

  The justice then came and, though grave was his look,
  Seemed to wish I would kiss him instead of the book,
  He whispered his clerk then and, leaving the place,
  I was had to his chamber to open the case.
      He pressed me &c.

  I went to our parson to make my complaint;
  He looked like a Bacchus, but preached like a saint.
  He said we should soberly Nature refresh,
  Then nine times he urged me to humble the flesh.
      He pressed me &c.

                    Penkethman's Jests, 1721

108 Early in the dawning of a winter's morn
  Brother Dick and I went forth into the barn,
          To get ourselves a heat

99

By threshing of the wheat
From the stack, from the stack, from the stack, the
stack.
The straws they flew about
And the flails they kept a rout,
With a thwack, thwack, thwack, thwack, thwack.

Margery came in then with an earthen pot,
Full of pudding that was piping hot;
I caught her by the neck fast
And thanked her for my breakfast,
With a smack, with a smack, with a smack, a smack.
Then up went her tail
And down went the flail,
With a thwack, thwack, thwack, thwack, thwack.

Dick, threshing on, cried out, 'Fie, for shame!
Must I beat the bush while you catch the game?
Sow your wild oats
And mind not her wild notes
Of alack, of alack, of alack, alack.'
Faith, I did the job,
While the flail bore a bob,
With a thwack, thwack, thwack, thwack, thwack.

She shook off the straws and did nothing ail,
Swearing there was no defence against a flail,
But quietly lay still
And bid me fill, fill, fill
Her sack, her sack, her sack, her sack;
But 'twas all in vain,
For I had spilt my grain
With a thwack, thwack, thwack, thwack, thwack.

*Wit and Mirth: or, Pills to
Purge Melancholy,* **1699-1700**

V

Lucy   Lord, madam, I met your lover in as much haste
as if he had been going for a midwife!

Silvia   He's going for a parson, girl, the forerunner of a
midwife, some nine months hence.

THE OLD BACHELOR

109 Maids are grown so coy of late
     Forsooth they will not marry;
     Though they are in their teens and past,
     They say they yet can tarry;
     But if they knew how sweet a thing
     It is in youth to marry,
     They then would sell their hose and smock
     Ere they so long would tarry.

     Winter nights are long, you know,
     And bitter cold the weather,
     Then who's so fond to lie alone
     When two may lie together?
     And is't not brave when summer comes,
     With all the fields enrolled,
     To take a green gown on the grass
     And wear it uncontrolled?

     For she that is most coy of all,
     If she had time and leisure,
     Would lay aside severest thoughts
     And turn to mirth and pleasure;
     For why the fairest maid sometimes
     Puts on the face of folly,
     And maids do ne'er repent so much
     As when they are too holy.

                              Penkethman's Jests, 1721

110 Since we poor slavish women know
     Our men we cannot pick and choose,
     To him we love we say him no
     And both our time and labour lose;
     By our put-offs and fond delays
     A lover's appetite we pall,

And if too long the gallant stays
His stomach's gone for good and all.

Or our impatient amorous guest,
Unknown to us, away may steal
And rather than stay for a feast
Take up with some coarse, homely meal.
When opportunity is kind
Let prudent woman be so too,
And if the man be to her mind
Be sure she do not let him go.

The match soon made is happiest still,
For Love has only there to do;
Let no one marry 'gainst her will,
But stand off when her parents woo;
And to the suitor be not coy,
For she whom jointure can obtain
To let a fop her bed enjoy
Is but a lawful wench for gain.

Reuben Bourne

111 From the temple to the board,
From the board unto the bed,
We conduct your maidenhead,
Wishing Hymen to afford
All the pleasures that he can
'Twixt a woman and a man.
    So merrily, merrily we pass along
    With our joyful, with our joyful bridal song.

Windsor Drollery, 1672

112 So now we have done the work of the day,
For the work of the night come all hands away —

To lay the sweet bride
By the bridegroom's side.
To bed, to bed with the bride.

Elkanah Settle

113 Tush! never tell me I'm too young
For loving or too green;
She stays at least sev'n years too long
That's wedded at eighteen:
Lambs bring forth lambs and doves bring doves
As soon as they're begotten,
Then why should ladies linger loves
As if not ripe till rotten?

Grey hairs are fitter for the grave
Than for the bridal bed;
What pleasure can a lover have
In a withered maidenhead?
Nature's exalted in our time,
And what our grandams then
At four and twenty scarce could climb
We can arrive at ten.

Sir Charles Sedley

114 *Prince George of Denmark*
While I in the camp
Was playing my part,
For Cupid and Venus
I cared not a fart.

Princess Anne
While I in the forest
Was looking birds' nests,
I thought not on Hymen

104

Or Love in the least;
But while I with Delia
  Up and down strayed,
I was in my conscience
  A very good maid.

Prince   Now Venus has tamed me
  With usage so coarse
That I vow I'm not able
  To get on my horse.

Princess   Why, to tell you the truth,
  I'm hurt i' th' same place
By another guise arrow
  Than Delia's was;
And Delia now can
  Do me no more good,
For what are her arrows
  To flesh and to blood?

Prince   But thou, when I smuggle thee,
  Smell'st so of balsam
That I am e'en ravished
  To think thou 'rt so wholesome:
My brother, King Kittern,
  While thou art my charge,
Is e'en a poor wretch
  Compared to Prince George.

Princess   And when thou but settest
  One foot in my bed,
I fancy my sister
  Is not so well sped;
Let her, with his flannel,
  Her Billy enjoy,

While none shall to Nanny
    Be dearer than thee.

Oh, happy, thrice happy
    Whom Love hath thus joined!
May such days and nights
    No period find!

Dyce MS. 43

115   Said Phillida,
            Said Phillida
    To Coridon, 'Let us be merry.'
            Then Coridon,
            Then Coridon
    Said, 'Come, let us over the ferry.

            On the other side
            I'll make thee my bride,
    And then, with the bottle of leather,
            With the neighbouring swains
            We'll dance on the plains
    And fuddle and frolic together.

            There I'll kiss thee
            And then caper
    While my blood does grow warmer and warmer,
    Then the lasses shall sing us to town a.
            We'll do t' other feat
            When thee and I meet
    On a bed that is soft as the down a.'

Bristol Drollery, 1674

116 See how charming Caelia lies upon her bridal bed;
     There's no such beauty at Court:

She's fit for the sport
And she looks so lovely, white and red.
After the first and second time
The bridegroom 'gins to slack his pace,
But she cries, 'Come, come, come, come to me
And lay thy cheek close to my face.'
Tinkle, tinkle, ting goes the bell to the bed
Whilst common time they keep;
   With a parting kiss
   They end their bliss
And so retire to sleep.

Wit and Mirth, 1682

117   Half her swelling breast
Naked met his, under the flowing gold
Of her loose tresses hid. He, in delight
Both of her beauty and submissive charms,
Smiled with superior love, as Jupiter
On Juno smiles when he impregns the clouds
That shed May flowers, and pressed her matron lip
With kisses pure. Aside the Devil turned
For envy . . . .

John Milton

118 Come from the temple away to the bed
   As the merchant transports home his treasure.
Be not so coy, lady, since we are wed
   'Tis no sin to taste of the pleasure.
     Then come, let us be
     Blithe, merry and free;
Upon my life, all the waiters are gone
     And 'tis so
     That they know

Where you go.
Say not so,
For I mean to make bold with my own.

What is it to me, though our hands joined be,
If our bodies be still kept asunder?
Shall it be said, 'There goes a married maid?'
Indeed we will have no such wonder.
Therefore let's embrace;
There's none sees thy face:
The bride-maids that waited are gone;
None can spy
How you lie.
Ne'er delay,
But say ay;
For I mean to make bold with my own.

Then come, let us kiss and taste of that bliss
Which lords and ladies have enjoyed;
If maidens should be of the humour of thee
Generations would soon be destroyed;
Then where were those joys,
The girls and the boys?
Wouldst live in the world all alone?
Don't destroy,
But enjoy;
Seem not coy
For a toy,
For I mean to make bold with my own.

Sweet love, do not frown, but put off thy gown:
'Tis a garment unfit for the night.
Some say that black hath a relishing smack;
I had rather be dealing in white.
Then be not afraid,

For you are not betrayed,
Since we are together alone;
    I invite
    You this night
    To do right,
    My delight—
'Tis forthwith to make bold with my own.

Prithee begin, don't delay, but unpin,
    For my humour I cannot prevent it.
You are strait laced and your gorget's so fast —
    Undo it or I straight will rend it,
      Or to end all the strife
      I'll cut it with my knife.
'Tis too long to stay till 'tis undone:
    Let thy waist
    Be unlaced
    And in haste
    Be embraced,
For I do long to make bold with my own.

Feel with your hand how you make me to stand,
    Even ready to starve with the cold.
Oh, why shouldst thou be so hard-hearted to me,
    That love thee more dearer than gold?
      And as thou hast been
      Like fair Venus the Queen,
Most pleasant in thy parts every one,
    Let me find
    That thy mind
    Is inclined
    To be kind,
So that I may make bold with my own.

As thou art fair and more sweet than the air

That dallies on July's brave roses,
Now let me be to that garden a key
    That the flowers of virgins incloses;
        And I will not be
        Too rough unto thee,
Though my nature unto boldness is prone.
        Do no less
        Than undress
        And unlace
        All apace,
For this night I'll make use of my own.

When I have found thee temperate and sound,
    Thy sweet breast I will make for my pillow.
'Tis pity that we, which newly married be,
    Shall be forced to wear the green willow;
        And we shall be blest
        And live sweetly at rest
Now we are united in one,
        With content
        And consent.
        I am bent,
        My intent
Is this night to make bold with my own.

Wit's Cabinet, circa 1700

119 Welcome, dear love. All the powers above
        Are well pleased at our happy meeting:
The Heavens have decreed and the Earth agreed
        That I should embrace my own sweeting;
                At bed and at board,
                Both in deed and in word,
My affections to thee shall be shown.
                Thou art mine,

110

I am thine;
Let us join
And combine:
I'd not bar thee from what is thy own.

Our bride-bed's made; thou shalt be my comrade,
    For to lodge in my arms all the night,
Where thou shalt enjoy, being free from annoy,
    All the sports wherein Love takes delight:
            Our mirth shall be crowned
            And our triumph renowned.
Then, sweetheart, let thy valour be shown;
            Take thy fill,
            Do thy will,
            Use thy skill,
            Welcome still.
Why shouldst thou not make bold with thy own?

The bridegroom and bride, with much joy on each side,
    Then together to bed they did go;
But what they did there I did neither see nor hear,
    Nor I do not desire to know,
            But by Cupid's aid
            They being well laid,
They made sport by themselves all alone;
            Being placed,
            And unlaced,
            He uncased,
            She embraced,
Then he stoutly made bold with his own.

Wit's Cabinet, circa 1700

120 *The bride and bridegroom both were gone to bed,*
Expecting each to lose their maidenhead;

The stocking being flung and the sack-posset eat,
Now bride and bridegroom must each other treat.
All being withdrawn and left them to their rest
The bridegroom thus to's bride his mind expressed:

Bridegroom
'Tis now, my dear, high time to storm the mint
Of love and joy, and rifle all that's in't.

Bride
No, my dear spouse, you'll find me far more tender:
You shall not need to storm, for I'll surrender;
For since i' th' temple my consent I've shown,
The pleasures I can yield you are your own.

Bridegroom
Since you will be so kind to yield up all,
I'll quickly make my joys reciprocal;
And not to lose more time, I'll now begin,
If you'll be pilot and conduct me in.

Bride
I will, but this request must granted be:
Deal gently, and then leave the rest to me.

Bridegroom
Fear not, my dear, my wits are not so slender
To use with roughness one that's young and tender.

Both thus agreed, they both were soon possessed
Of joys too great, too vast to be expressed.

                    Wit's Cabinet, circa 1700

121 To bed ye two in one united go,
               To pleasure's killing;
     Embrace and struggle till your spirits flow,

112

Embrace more willing
Than th' loving palms (great union's wonder)
    That ne'er bore any fruit asunder.

Be young to each when winter and grey hairs
                Your head shall clime;
May your affections like the merry spheres
                Still move in time,
And may (with many a good presage)
    Your marriage prove your merry age.

Wit at a Venture, 1674

122 *To The Bride on the Bride-Night:—*

*Lady, may all the joys of Hymen's sacred bands
this night attend you.*

*Dear Mrs Bride, may all the joys of love and
innocence this night be yours.*

Now, Mrs Bride, that we must take our leave,
May you the confluence of all joys receive.

And as for you, sir, you may storm the mint
Of love and joy, and rifle all that's in't.

Wit's Cabinet, circa 1700

123 Where's my shepherd, my love? hey-ho,
    On yonder mountain amidst the snow,
I dearly love him, I vow, and now
    Will follow and merrily to him go:
My young shepherd has beauty and charms
And I long to find him in my arms;
I long for night to embrace him abed
And I long to give him my maidenhead.

Soft and sweet are the joys of love,
    Which every virgin does long to prove;
I will not tarry, but marry,
    And every rival will soon remove.
Bonny Susan doth muse on all night
Upon all our joys and sweet delight;
She dreams of kisses, embraces and charms,
And she starts and thinks her love in her arms.

Sweetly looks the fair bride in bed
    With thousand Cupids all round her head;
She softly sighs and wishes and kisses,
    As soon as the curtains are closely spread.
Every bridegroom does then what he please
And the lovely brides their flames appease;
I need not name what young lovers do do,
For 'tis known to everyone, aye, and to you.

Mark how kindly she looks next day,
    More lively, lovely, more brisk and gay;
'T would make maids long to be cooing and wooing,
    To see how these wantons do sport and play.
Some new charm in his looks she espies,
And then he looks babies in her eyes;
Then while her fondling new pleasures does seek,
She kindly kisses and claps his cheek.

Vain it is to be nice and coy
    And let old Time all our youth destroy:
I like not whining and pining
    For that which one easily might enjoy;
There are bonny, brisk lovers in store,
And then what can maidens wish for more?
What need has Susan to sigh and look pale,
When she might o'er Thomas his heart prevail?

Have not women soft charms and arts
   By Nature given to conquer hearts,
Which never does fail, but prevail
   As often as ever they shoot their darts?
No brisk youth can withstand a maid's charms,
But does strangely soften in her arms;
The roughest hero in all the bright field
To a brighter beauty will bow and yield.

Now young buxom, fair maids, come here
   And learn this lesson. To Love give ear;
The little boy is so pretty and witty
   And pleasant and soft that you need not fear.
Roger he shall have Cisley and Nan,
And young Kate shall kiss my ladies' man;
Doll shall have William and John shall have Joan;
And thus neither sex shall lie alone.

Broadside, circa 1685

124   Were I to take wife
         (As 'tis for my life)
She should be brisk, pleasant and merry:
         A lovely fine brown,
         A face all her own,
With a lip red and round as a cherry;

         Not much of the wise,
         Less of the precise,
Nor over-reserved nor yet flying;
         Hard breasts, a straight back,
         An eye full and black,
But languishing as she were dying.

         And then for her dress,
         Be't more or be't less,

Not tawdry set out, nor yet meanly;
    And one thing beside,
    Just, just so much pride
As may serve to keep honest and cleanly.

John Wilson

125 If thou wilt know how to choose a shrew,
    Come listen unto me:
I'll tell you the signs and the very, very lines
    Of Love's physiognomy.

If her hair be brown, with a flaxen crown,
    And graced with a nutmeg hue,
Both day and night she's best for delight
    And her colour everlasting true.

If her forehead be high, with a rolling eye,
    And lips that will sweetly melt,
The thing below is better, you know,
    Although it be oftener felt.

If her hair be red she'll sport in the bed,
    But take heed of the danger, though;
For if she carry fire in her upper attire,
    What a divel doth she carry below?

If her hair be yellow, she'll tempt each Fellow
    In the Emmanuel College;
For she that doth follow the colour of Apollo
    May be like him in zeal of knowledge.

If she be pale and a virgin stale,
    Inclined to the sickness green,
Some raw fruit give her to open her liver,
    Her stomach and the thing between.

If her nose be long and sharp as her tongue,
    Take heed of a desperate maid;
For she that will swagger with an incurable dagger
    With stab and a killing betrayed.

If her face and neck have here and there a speck,
    Ne'er stick, but straight you go stride her;
For it hath been tried, and never denied,
    Such flesh ne'er fails the rider.

If none of these thy fancy will please,
    Go seek thy complexion store,
And take for thy saint a lady that will paint:
    Such beauties thou may'st adore.

If beauty do write in her face red and white
    And Cupid his flowers there breed,
It pleaseth the eye, but the rose will die
    As soon as it runs to seed.

Merry Drollery Complete, 1691

126 'Twas when the sheep were shearing
    And under the barley-mow,
Dick gave to Doll a fairing
    As she had milked her cow.
Quoth he, 'I fain would wed thee
    And though I cannot woo,
I've hey pish, hey cock, hey, and hey for a boy,
Sing, shall I come kiss thee now?
    Ah, shall I come, shall I come kiss thee now?
I long, sweetheart, to wed thee
    And merrily buckle to,
With a hey pish &c.
Sing, shall I come kiss thee now?
    Sing, ah, shall &c.'

Doll seemed not to regard him,
    As if she did not care,
Yet simpered when she heard him
    Like any miller's mare,
And cunningly to prove him
    And value her maidenhead,
Cried, 'Fie, nay pish, nay fie, and prithee stand by,
    For I am too young to wed.'
She said she ne'er could love him
    Nor any man else in bed:
'Then fie, pish fie, nay pish, nay prithee stand by,
    For I am too young to wed.'

Like one that's struck with thunder
    Stood Dicky to hear her talk;
All hopes to get her under
    This sad resolve did baulk.
At last he swore, grown bolder,
    He'd hire some common sow,
For hey pish, hey cock &c.
    Sing &c.
    Sing shall I come, shall I come to kiss thee now?
In loving arms did fold her,
    Ere sneak and cringe and cry
With a hey pish, hey cock, hey, hey for a boy
    Sing &c.
Sing &c.

Convinced of her coy folly
    And stubborn female will,
Poor Dolly grew melancholy;
    The grist went by her mill.
'I hope,' she cried, 'you're wiser
    Than credit what I have said,
Though I cry, "Nay fie, and pish, and prithee stand by,"

That I am too young to wed.
Bring you the church-adviser
　　And dress the bridal bed,
Then try, though I cry "Fie," and "Prithee stand by,"
　　If I am too young to wed,
　　If I am too, I am too young to wed.'

Wit's Cabinet, circa 1700

127　At Winchester was a wedding,
　　　The like was never seen,
　　Twixt lusty Ralph of Redding
　　　And bonny Bess of the Green;
　　The fiddlers were crowding before,
　　　Each lass was as fine as a queen;
　　There was a hundred and more,
　　　For all the country came in.
　　Brisk Robin led Rose so fair,
　　　She looked like a lily o'th' vale;
　　And ruddy-faced Harry led Mary
　　　And Roger led bouncing Nell.

　　With Tommy came smiling Katy;
　　　He helped her over the stile
　　And swore there was none so pretty
　　　In forty and forty long mile.
　　Kit gave a green gown to Betty
　　　And lent her his hand to rise;
　　But Jenny was jeered by Watty
　　　For looking blue under the eyes.
　　Thus merrily chatting all
　　　They passed to the bride-house along,
　　With Johnny and pretty-faced Nancy,
　　　The fairest of all the throng.

　　The bridegroom came out to meet 'em,

119

Afraid the dinner was spoiled,
And ushered 'em in to treat 'em
    With baked and roasted and boiled.
The lads were so frolic and jolly,
    For each had his love by his side;
But Willy was melancholy,
    For he had a mind to the bride.
Then Philip begins her health
    And turns a beer glass on his thumb,
But Jenkin was reckoned for drinking
    The best in Christendom.

And now they had dined, advancing
    Into the midst of the hall,
The fiddlers struck up for dancing
    And Jeremy led up the brawl;
But Margery kept a quarter
    (A lass that was proud of herself)
'Cause Arthur had stolen her garter
    And swore he would tie it himself;
She struggled and blushed and frowned
    And ready with anger to cry,
'Cause Arthur with tying her garter
    Had slipped his hand too high.

And now for throwing the stocking
    The bride away was led;
The bridegroom got drunk and was knocking
    For candles to light 'em to bed;
But Robin, that found him silly,
    Most friendly took him aside,
The while that his wife with Willy
    Was playing at hooper's hide.
And now the warm game begins,
    The critical minute was come,

120

And chatting and billing and kissing
   Went merrily round the room.

Pert Stephen was kind to Betty
   And blithe as a bird in the spring;
And Tommy was so to Katy
   And wedded her with a rush ring.
Sukey, that danced with the cushion,
   An hour from the room had been gone,
And Barnaby knew by her blushing
   That some other dance had been done;
And thus of fifty fair maids
   That came to the wedding with men
Scarce five of the fifty was left ye
   That so did return again.

Wit and Mirth: or, Pills to
Purge Melancholy, 1699 − 1700

128   When for air
              I take my mare
           And mount her, first
              She walks just thus:
           Her head held low
              And motion slow,
           With nodding, plodding,
              Wagging, jogging,
           Dashing, plashing,
              Snorting, starting
           Whimsically she goes,
           Then whip stirs up,
              Trot, trot, trot.
           Ambling then with easy flight,
           She wriggles like a bird at night;

Her shifting hitch
　　Regales my britch,
Whilst trot, trot, trot, trot
　　Brings on the gallop,
The gallop, the gallop,
The gallop, and then a short
　　Trot, trot, trot, trot
Straight again up and down,
　　Up and down, up and down,
Till she comes home with a trot,
When night dark grows.

Just so Phillis
　　Fair as lilies
As her face is,
　　Has her paces;
And in bed too,
　　Like my pad too,
Nodding, plodding,
　　Wagging, jogging,
Dashing, plashing,
　　Flirting, spurting;
Artful are all her ways −
　　Hearts thump, pit pat,
　　Trot, trot, trot, trot.
Ambling then her tongue gets loose,
Whilst wriggling near I press more close.
　　'Ye devil!' she cries,
　　'I'll tear your eyes'.
When, mane seized,
　　Bum squeezed,
I gallop, I gallop, I gallop, I gallop,
　　And trot, trot, trot, trot,
Straight again up and down,
Up and down, up and down,

Till the last jerk, with a trot,
Ends our love chase.

Wit and Mirth: or, Pills to
Purge Melancholy, 1699 – 1700

129   A gentlewoman sitting carelessly by a fireside
sat straddling. Her husband, in a pleasant humour,
told her that her cabinet stood open. 'Say you so?'
said she. 'Why don't you lock it then? For I am sure
that none keeps the key but yourself.'

Nugae Venales, 1686

130 My young Mary does mind the dairy
While I go a hoeing and mowing each morn;
Then hey the little spinning-wheel
Merrily round does reel,
        While I am singing amidst the corn.
Cream and kisses both are my delight;
She gives me them and the joys of night;
She's soft as the air, as morning fair.
Is not such a maid a most pleasing sight?

While I whistle she from the thistle
Does gather down for to make us a bed;
And there my little love does lie
All the night long and die
        In the kind arms of her own dear Ned.
Then I taste of a delicate spring
But I mun not tell you, nor name the thing,
To put you a wishing and think of kissing;
For kisses cause sighs and young men should sing.

Broadside, circa 1685

VI

Her husband out of Town and she alone. — This had
ı a time. — hah, what room's that, what's there? A
h laid, knives, napkins, oranges and bread. — Late
t is, here will be a supper, all this preparation cannot
or tomorrow, somebody is to come in the husband's
nce, . . .

THE LONDON CUCKOLDS

131　　A bridegroom the first night he was in bed with his bride said unto her, 'Whenas at such time I solicited thy chastity, hadst thou then condescended I would never have made thee my wife, for I did it only to try thee.' 'Faith,' said she, 'I did imagine as much, but I had been cozened so three or four times before and I was resolved to be cozened no more.'

Nugae Venales, 1686

132 Woman, who is by nature wild,
　　Dull, bearded man incloses;
Of Nature's freedom we're beguiled
　　By laws which man imposes,
Who still himself continues free,
Yet we poor slaves must fettered be.

Chorus
　　　　　A shame on the curse
　　　　　Of 'For better, for worse':
'Tis a vile imposition on Nature;
　　　　　For women should change
　　　　　And have freedom to range,
Like to every other wild creature.

So gay a thing was ne'er designed
　　To be restrained from roving;
Heaven meant so changeable a mind
　　Should have its change in loving.
By cunning we could make men smart,
But they by strength o'ercome our art.

Chorus　　A shame on the curse, *etc.*

How happy is the village maid,
　　Whom only Love can fetter;

By foolish Honour ne'er betrayed
　　She serves a power much greater:
That lawful prince the wisest rules,
The usurper's Honour rules but fools.

Chorus　　A shame on the curse *etc.*

Let us resume our ancient right,
　　Make man at distance wonder;
Though he victorious be in fight,
　　In love we'll keep him under.
War and ambition hence be hurled,
Let Love and Beauty rule the world.

Chorus　　A shame on the curse *etc.*

Thomas Shadwell

133　　A young man married a pretty, buxom young
woman in Charenton near Paris, and being in bed
the first night, he let a rousing fart. His new bedded
comfort, very much displeased thereat, asked him
why he would offer so soon to play the beast. 'Alas,
sweetheart,' said he, 'don't you know, when a fortress
is besieged, in making a breach the cannons will
roar?' 'In troth, husband,' said she, 'you need not
have put yourself to that trouble, for the breach was
made long ago, wide enough for a whole army to
enter two in a breast.'

Nugae Venales, 1686

134　　　　Join and curse the tie with me
　　　　　That confines us to one bed:
　　　　This alone you can agree —

Cursed be he, cursed be he, cursed be he that made
you wed!

Peter Motteux

135 In the Fields of Lincoln's Inn,
    Underneath a woollen blanket,
    On a flock-bed, God be thanked,
Feats of active love were seen.

Phillis, who, you know, loves swiving
    As the Gods love pious prayers,
Lay most pensively contriving
    How to use her pricks by pairs.

Corydon's aspiring tarse,
    Which to cunt had near submitted,
    Wet with amorous kiss she fitted
To her less frequented arse.

Strephon's was a handful longer,
    Stiffly propped with eager lust —
In Love's wars no champion stronger —
    This into her cunt she thrust.

Now for civil wars prepare,
    Raised by fierce intestine bustle,
    When these heroes meeting justle
In the bowels of the fair.

They tilt and thrust with horrid pudder;
    Blood and slaughter is decreed,
Hurling souls at one another
    Wrapt in flaky clots of seed.

Nature had 'twixt cunt and arse
    Wisely placed firm separation.

God knows else what desolation
Had ensued from warring tarse.

Nor did th'event of what we treat on
    Happen worse than was desired:
The nymph was sorely ballock beaten,
    Both the shepherds soundly tired.

Royal Library, Stockholm, MS
Vu 69

136 1.   Boy, call the coach. Come, Jack, let's away;
            'Tis tedious to sit out this tragical play.
            A plague o'their plotting and dying in rhyme:
                            Let's drive to the Park
                            Before it be dark;
            There we'll better dispose of our time.

    2.   Stay, who is that so dressed like a queen?

    1.   'Tis the fine Lady Lofty, but let's not be seen,
            For her husband is surely gone out.

Chorus
                            She searches to find
                            If a friend will be kind
            And treat her abroad with a supper and bout.

    2.   Why should she want that? Her lord's a brave man.

    1.   Ay, Jack, but they're married.

    2.   Then what two are yon?

    1.   'Tis Will Lovewell and his pretty miss;
            He hath kept her this seven year, yet prithee
                            Jack, see

How jocund and merry
they be,
How crowned and en-
circled with bliss.

Chorus
    Love revels and feasts in hearts that are free,
    But languishing starves if restrainèd he be.

1.   See, yonder sits Well-born with his pretty wife.

2.   They look as they'd ne'er seen each other before.

1.   She seeks for her gallant, and he, o' my life,
    Hath a mind to be feaguing yon vizor-mask-whore
    But stay, let me see — by Heavens, 'tis so!
    That mask hides a lady I know,
    Who seems for to dote on husband and honour,
    But look there, Ned Ranter has just fixed upon her.

2.   She hath yielded, and see, they do go.

1.   If wives will do this,
                        Give me the true miss—
    She'd be hanged ere she'd serve a man so.

Chorus
    They're fools then that marry and strive to
                              confine
    In politic chains what still will be free:
    No fetters can hold a power that's divine,
    Nor shackles restrain great Love's Deity.

                    Henry Nevil Payne

137 What fortune had I, poor maid as I am,
     To be bound in eternal vow

Forever to lie by the side of a man
   That would, but knows not how!
       Oh! can there no pity
       Be in such a city
Where lads enough are to be had?

Unfortunate girl that art wed to such woe,
   Go, seek thee a lively lad,
And let the poor that hath nothing to show
   Go seek for another as bad.
       Then call for no pity;
       Thou dwelt in a city
Where lads enough were to be had.

               An Antidote against Melancholy,
                          1661

138 *Mrs Gosnell*   Ah, Love is a delicate ting,
                   Ah, Love is a delicate ting;
                   In Vinter it gives de new Spring.

    Chorus   It makes de dull Dush vor to dance
                   Nimbell as Monsieur of France.

    Mrs Gosnell   Ande dough it often does make,
                   Ande dough it often does make,
                   De head of de cuckol to ache,

    Chorus   Yet let him bute vinke at de lover
                   And de paine vill quickly be over.

    Mrs Gosnell   De husband must still vink a littel,
                   De husband must still vink a littel
                   Ande sometime be blinde as a bee-tell.

    Chorus   Ande de vife too sometime must be,

Ven he play trick, as blinde as he.

Sir William Davenant

139   *A cheesemonger's wife went astray*
      And with her own prentice did play:
        Her husband she horned
        And his company scorned,
     But Johnny was her pretty boy.

Mistress   Here's a health to my cuckold abed,
        To the horns thou hast put upon's head;
          So we have our delight
          All day and all night,
        Let him drink till his nose looks red.

John   My mistress' good health I'll begin
        And my glass shall be filled to the brim;
          With her for to lie
          I will never deny:
        To be kind I do count it no sin.

John and his Mistress,
circa 1680

140 My master with needle and thimble
    Must take his stitches so nimble,
        Else he'll be made poor
        By his wife, that young whore,
    For she longs to play with a wimble.

    Yet in troth I cannot her blame,
    For my master is both old and lame;
        Was I in her place,
        In spite of disgrace,

Without doubt I should do the same.

*A Merry Dialogue between Tom the
Tailor and his Maid Joan,* 1684

141 *Titere Tu*
Let him alone and you won't be rid of him. He's
like the blind beggars of Bolonia: a man must give
'em a halfpenny to sing and twopence to hold their
tongues.

Bilboe (sings)
Come, give the wench that is mellow,
And a pox take all fools that are yellow:
   'Tis the horn, the horn,
   The advancing of the horn,
Dubs a cuckold an alderman's fellow.

Let no man disorder his rest
By believing bull's feathers in's crest:
   When you've said what you can
   A cuckold is a man,
Or most of our fathers were beasts.

Then let us sing at it and at it,
And let ev'ryone catch that can catch it.
   All opinions agree
   In one of these three:
The horn, the pot or the placket.

         John Wilson

142 Smug, rich and fantastic, an old fumbler was known
 That wedded a juicy, brisk girl of the town,
  Her face like an angel, fair, plump and a maid,
   Her lute well in tune, too, if he could have played;

But lost was his skill; let him do what he can,
　She finds him in bed a poor, silly old man.
He coughs in her ear: ''Tis in vain to come on.
　Forgive me, my dear, I'm a silly old man.'

He laid his dry hand on her snowy soft breast
　And from those white hills gave a glimpse of the
　　　　　　　　　　　　　　　　　　　best,
But oh, what is Age, when our youth's but a span?
　She found him an infant instead of a man.
'Ah! pardon,' he cried, 'that I'm weary so soon:
　You have let down my base, I'm no longer in tune.
Lay by the dear instrument, prithee be still;
　I can play but one lesson, and that I play ill.'

Penkethman's Jests, 1721

143　　　　How blest was the created state
　　　　　　　Of man and woman, ere they fell,
　　　　　Compared to our unhappy fate:
　　　　　　　We need not fear another hell.

　　　　　Naked beneath cool shades they lay;
　　　　　　　Enjoyment waited on desire;
　　　　　Each member did their wills obey,
　　　　　　　Nor could a wish set pleasure higher.

　　　　　But we, poor slaves to hope and fear,
　　　　　　　Are never of our joys secure;
　　　　　They lessen still as they draw near,
　　　　　　　And none but dull delights endure.

　　　　　Then, Chloris, while I duly pay
　　　　　　　The nobler tribute of my heart,
　　　　　Be not you so severe to say

You love me for the frailer part.
John Wilmot, Earl of Rochester

144   The Hunt is up!
The Hunt is up!
And now it is almost day,
And he that's abed with another man's wife,
It's time to get him away.

Merry Drollery Complete, 1691

145   Let scenes of mirth and love,
    With songs and dances joining,
The fleeting hours improve
    And banish dull repining.
He who these joys refuses,
    When kindly they invite,
The end of living loses;
    Life's business is delight.

Peter Motteux

INDEX OF AUTHORS,
ANONYMOUS WORKS,
PRINTED MISCELLANIES
AND MANUSCRIPTS

*   Indicates that the item is abridged.

†   This poem by Oliver Le Neve is found in Chetham MS.
      Mun. A.4.14. a collection of verse by various hands
      which he himself transcribed. For biographical details
      of Le Neve see R.W. Ketton-Cremer: *Norfolk Portraits*,
      London, 1944, pp. 58-68.